Museum Volunteers

Museum Volunteers

Good Practice in the Management of Volunteers

Sinclair Goodlad
and
Stephanie McIvor

London and New York

First published 1998
by Routledge
11 New Fetter Lane, London EC4P 4EE

© 1998 Sinclair Goodlad and Stephanie McIvor

Typeset in Sabon by Keystroke, Jacaranda Lodge, Wolverhampton
Printed and bound in Great Britain by TJ International Ltd, Padstow, Cornwall

British Library Cataloguing in Publication Data
A catalogue record for this book is available from the British Library

Library of Congress Cataloguing in Publication Data
A catalog record for this book has been requested

ISBN 0–415–18209–3

Contents

6340

Acknowledgements

It is a pleasure to acknowledge the help of the many people who assisted us in the work that led to the production of this book.

First thanks must go to the Trustees of the Nuffield Foundation, who funded the collaborative Science Interpretation Project between Imperial College and the Science Museum (London), and the Director of the Nuffield Foundation, Mr Anthony Tomei, for his personal advice. John Durant, Assistant Director of the Science Museum, and Professor of the Public Understanding of Science at Imperial College, helped in formulating the bid for funds, and served on the steering group.

A steering group with specialists from the museum field, the voluntary sector and academia oversaw the progress of the project. The following served as members of this group during the course of the project: Ms Betty Caplan, Pimlico Connection Co-ordinator (to 31 January 1996); Ms Lisa Conway, Training and Development Executive, Museum Training Institute; Mr Graham Driver, Head of Science and Mathematics, Holland Park School; Professor John Durant, Assistant Director, the Science Museum (London) (to 31 December 1994); Dr Graham Farmelo, Head of Programmes, the Science Museum (London) (from 1 January 1995); Ms Margaret Greaves, Head of Training and Information, South Eastern Museum Service; Professor Richard Gregory, founder of the Bristol Exploratory; Mr Adrian Hawksworth, Pimlico Connection Co-ordinator (from 1 February 1996); Mr John Hughes, Project Manager, BP International Mentoring and Tutoring Project; Professor Arthur Lucas, Principal, King's College London; Ms Jan Metcalfe, Programmes Manager, the Science Museum (London) (from 30 June 1995); Professor David Phillips, Head of the Chemistry Department, Imperial College; Mr John Potter, Head of Education, Community Service Volunteers. Their advice was indispensable at crucial stages of the project.

We received copious information, and much help, from the following institutions to whom we are most grateful (alphabetically by institution): in Canada – Ontario Science Center; Science North, Sudbury, Ontario; University of Toronto School of Continuing Studies. In the United States of America – Boston Children's Museum; Museum of Science, Boston; The California Academy of

Science, San Francisco; Chicago Museum of Science and Industry; COSI Ohio's Center of Science and Industry, Columbus; Denver Museum of Natural History; Evansville Museum of Arts and Science, Indiana; the Exploratorium, San Francisco; Field Museum of Natural History, Chicago; Fort Worth Museum of Science and History, Texas; The Franklin Institute, Philadelphia; Lakeview Museum of Arts and Sciences, Peoria, Illinois; Louisville Science Center, Louisville, Kentucky; McKinley Museum of History, Science, and Industry, Canton, Ohio; The New England Acquarium, Boston; The Oakland Museum of California; The Smithsonian Institution, Washington, DC; St. Louis Science Center, St. Louis, Missouri; The State Historical Society of Colorado. In the United Kingdom – The Archaeological Resource Centre, York; Kew Bridge Steam Museum, London; London Transport Museum; London Zoo; Museum of Transport, Manchester; The Museum of Science and Industry, Manchester; Museum of Transport, Glasgow; National Maritime Museum, London; National Railway Museum, York; Natural History Museum, London; People's Palace, Glasgow; Royal Air Force Museum, Hendon; The Scottish Fisheries Museum, Fife.

We owe special thanks to the following people who were particularly generous with their time, in some cases (those with asterisks) checking through our draft text concerning their institutions: Chris Allender, Carl Atkinson, Lesley Bosine, Ellen Calhoun, Christine Castle,* Sarah Christian,* Constance Demb,* Bobbie Dillon, John Freeborn, Michelle Gerlis, Beverley Hawley, Lesley Kennedy,* Lucy Kirshner,* Vijaya Kunar,* Judith Kupfer, Carold Lalande,* Marista Leishman, Michelle Lynch, Margaret McGloughlin, Michael Melia, Jane Necher, Kitty Pfutzenreuter, Joan Philips, Sue Shave, Magda Shremp, Aileen Smart, Ben Spencer, Dennis Wilkinson, Betsy Willcuts,* Bob Winger, and Diane Young.

Kogan Page kindly gave permission for us to use in Chapter Five material that first appeared in 'Students as museum interpreters', pp. 52–62 of *Students as Tutors and Mentors* (ed.) S. Goodlad (London: Kogan Page, 1995).

The burden of organising the Imperial College side of the joint pilot schemes fell upon successive co-ordinators of the Pimlico Connection – John C. Hughes, Betty Caplan and Adrian Hawksworth. Above all, the student tutors in the Pimlico Connection who helped to establish the initial programme, and the many volunteers who worked in the Science Museum (London) subsequently, were the people who 'made it all happen'. The latter were: Cian Allner, Sarah Awan, Mark Ayling, Natalie Clara Barb, Faye Baxter, Sally Baxter, Lucy Bear, Katie Bird, Catriona Brannan, Catherine Bristow, Laura Brooks, Tim Brown, Poppy Buxton, Nathan Robert Carr, Marion Clark, Victoria Cline, Teodora Constantinescu, Lindsay Cook, Helen Crowson, Kirsten Cyr, Henry Dare, Helen Jacqueline Dell, Sonya Elizabeth Dowsett, Janet Evans, Susan Fletcher, Simon Forster, Daniel Friesner, Samantha Fulker, John Bernard Gibson, Emily Goodlad, Stewart Green, Melissa Grintell, Nico Gubbins, Catherine Halcrow, Catherine Halliwell, Helen Hampton, Margaret Heather Hare, Rhian Harris, Gillian Heath, Laszlo Heckenast, Graeme Hoyle, John Hunnex, Zahoor

Hussain, Simon Hyde, Sharif Islaam, Lee Jackson, Jack Kane, Chong-Yee Khoo, Susan Klugman, Leon Kotze, Colin Ledsome, Stefan Lewandowski, Wee-Lin Lim, Charlotte Louise Mabey, Annabel Victoria Malins, Jason Manger, Peter Martin, David McCormack, Rosalind Mist, John Morley, Kay Nelson, Barry O'Brien, Patrick O'Donnell, Aireni Omerri, Albert Opoku, Melinda Maria Paine, Carolyn Parkin, Katherine Pilgrim, Libby Pink, Michael Profit, Nicola Pyne, Jenny Rees-Tonge, Frederique Rive, Santa Rivelli, Felicity Catherine Robertson, Helen Rosenbaum, Fiona Sampson, Christine Schuler, Louise Seymour, Mimeda Sharif, Salima Begum Shariff, Christine Shepherd, Jonathan Brian Silverman, Diane Slater, Josh Smith, Lorna Smith, Rachel Souhami, Lucy Stable, Maria Strangward, Dhiren Sutaria, Tadashi Suzuma, David Timney, Kenneth Tomory, Karin Tybjerg, Andres Varela, Elizabeth May Wakely, Claire Helene Walker, Steven Walsh, Helen Weaver, Mary Wessel, Claire Belinda White, and Philip Wilkin.

Finally, we owe a debt of gratitude to Victoria Peters, Commissioning Editor at Routledge, and to Andrew Wheatcroft the series editor, and to two anonymous referees, all of whom helped to improve the text.

Without the advice and practical activity of these people, the project would not have happened and the book would not have been written. We do, however, willingly exonerate them from responsibility for anything inaccurate that we have written.

Sinclair Goodlad and Stephanie McIvor

July 1997

Abbreviations

AAM	American Association of Museums
AAMV	American Association of Museum Volunteers
AGO	Art Gallery of Ontario
ASTC	Association of Science and Technology Centers (US)
BAFM	British Association of Friends of Museums
BAYSDAYS	British Association Youth Section Days
CDT	Craft Design Technology
CSV	Community Service Volunteers
GAGMA	Glasgow Art Gallery and Museums Association
ICOM	International Council of Museums
TUS	Trade Union Side
UGC	University Grants Committee (UK)
UNESCO	United Nations Educational, Scientific, and Cultural Organisation
UFT SCS	University of Toronto School of Continuing Studies
WFFM	World Federation of Friends of Museums

1

Making knowledge accessible

1.1 Introduction

The thesis of this book is that volunteers can make an effective and personally fulfilling contribution to museum interpretation and that the support of volunteers can be crucial in releasing the creative energies of hard-pressed, paid museum professionals.

The project from which this book arises was funded by the Nuffield Foundation of the United Kingdom which provided funding for two years (1994–6) to develop a scheme of volunteer interpreters in the Science Museum (London), (part of the National Museum for Science & Industry). It draws, *inter alia*, on work done in the neighbouring institution, the Imperial College of Science, Technology and Medicine in exploring for some 20 years the use of students as tutors and mentors (see Goodlad and Hirst, 1989, 1990; Goodlad 1995a, 1995b). The research on student tutoring has shown the many benefits that can accrue to students, the teachers with whom they work and the school pupils who are tutored; it also points up a number of issues that will need attention as interpretation by volunteers becomes established in museums and science centres. The most important of these is the role of the volunteer manager; for this reason, the Nuffield Science Interpretation Project has concentrated on exploring, by research and practical experiment, the task of managing volunteers.

The idea of museum interpretation by volunteers is a simple one, but one that is complex to put into practice. By bringing together two streams of research and development work, on tutoring by student volunteers and museum interpretation, the book examines principles of good practice and administrative procedures that will be needed whenever volunteers work alongside professionals in enhancing and extending the role of museums. Although the development work undertaken in the project focused on science, the issues discussed are relevant to museum interpretation in other fields too.

In leading towards the analysis of principles of good practice, the chapters that follow cover:

- the development of first-person interpretation work in museums;
- the development of student tutoring as a form of volunteering;
- case studies of exemplary programmes of interpretation by volunteers;
- case studies of pilot volunteer programmes in the Science Museum (London).

As a field of discourse, the notion of interpretation (and the multitude of activities that support it) is huge, encompassing theories of child education, adult education, exhibition design, and volunteering. This book, and the project funded by the Nuffield Foundation from which it flows, concentrates on the *management* of volunteer programmes. Our thesis is that if the management of volunteers is done well, a huge resource of interested, concerned and lively people can help to educate others and simultaneously educate themselves. They can also develop an aspect of our culture with which universities, colleges, schools, museums and science centres are deeply involved – drawing upon, and contributing to, the development of science.

To bring some of the key issues into focus, this first chapter touches on: the nature of interpretation; methods of making complex ideas intelligible; the aims and purposes of volunteering; and the aims of the Nuffield Science Interpretation Project of which this book is a product.

1.2 Museum interpretation: methods of making complex ideas intelligible

The key task of communicators, including those in science, is to locate new ideas in a frame of reference which is familiar and intelligible to the intended audience (see Goodlad, 1996: Chapter 3). We use this process in everyday discourse when we describe or define something. We start by placing the new item in the widest possible category of descriptors and then progressively differentiate it from all other items in that category until its distinguishing, unique or most interesting features are highlighted. (Try defining, for example, milk for someone who has never seen it or consumed it!) The communication of ideas is difficult to achieve through impersonal or mass processes because the communicator does not receive feedback from the person to whom ideas are communicated. By contrast, in a conversation the questions (or bewildered looks) of an interlocutor help the communicator to know when to re-cast the framework, progressively moving back from the particular to the wider frame of reference that resonates with, or has meaning for, the person concerned.

Science is sometimes believed to be more difficult to communicate than other subjects, but this need not necessarily be so. At the macro level, the process of communicating scientific ideas is relatively straightforward. It is not difficult to adduce reasons why we should be interested in science as a human activity (Goodlad, 1973). Modern culture is penetrated at every point by the insights and activities of scientists. Our technology is largely science-based; huge sums of the money we pay in taxes are used to support scientific research; our very perception of ourselves is largely a product of scientific insight; and so on.

Sociologists of science have little difficulty in demonstrating that the subject-matter of scientific enquiry, and indeed its very processes, are deeply interwoven with other ideas and social institutions (see, for example, Ravetz, 1971; Richter, 1973; Barnes and Edge, 1982; Ben-David, 1984; Barnes, 1985; Latour, 1987; Masters, 1993). There are, in short, numerous points of purchase whereby scientific ideas can be interpreted within a framework intelligible to lay people. Nevertheless, those interested in the public understanding of science believe much more needs to be done (Royal Society, 1985), and many difficult questions remain, such as these: Are there any defining features of science? Where should the process of interpretation begin? How does one use the products and appurtenances of scientific enquiry and technological adventuring to create a living experience that will simultaneously fire the imagination of the uninitiated and nourish the thinking of the specialist? Is it, in fact, impossible to do both of these things at once? What helps visitors to understand what they see? Such questions have excited interest for over 60 years (Melton, Feldman, and Mason, 1936) and continue to do so (Serrell, 1990, 1993; Bicknell and Farmelo, 1993).

At the cognitive level, the difficulty of communicating factual information and ideas through museum exhibits is well known: people do not seem to take in or remember much of what they passively see and hear (see Miles, 1987; Uzzell, 1993). Increasingly it is being realised that it is artificial to separate the cognitive and the affective (McManus, 1993), and attention is moving towards the totality of 'the museum experience' (Falk and Dierking, 1992). In the fields of science and technology there has been the rapid growth of interactive or 'hands-on' science centres. The Science Museum's Children's Gallery, developed in the 1930s with 'push-button' working models of machines (which was re-developed and re-opened in 1995 as 'The Basement' – a new suite of galleries, one of which targets a new audience of under-fives), became the inspiration for Frank Oppenheimer's San Francisco Exploratorium (opened in 1969) which pioneered the use of genuinely interactive exhibits whereby visitors could carry out experiments and see, hear, and feel phenomena directly. The object was, and is, to allow people to find things out for themselves – even by doing things incorrectly (Duensing, 1987: 140). In like manner, the Bristol Exploratory is designed, in the words of its founder Richard Gregory, to 'enrich our everyday perception by providing encounters with surprises' (Gregory, 1986: 18). (Science World, due to open in the year 2000 as part of the Bristol 2000 harbourside development, will replace the Bristol Exploratory.) Over the past 20 years, there has been a huge growth world-wide in this type of science centre (see, for example, Pizzey, 1987, Nuffield Foundation, 1989; Durant, 1992). Some conventional science and technology museums seem torn between their custodial and inspirational functions.

As we show in Chapter Two, differences in emphasis in the main functions of museums have been developing between those museums which concentrate on the collection, preservation and exhibition of important artefacts and those that seek to promote understanding and enjoyment of the process of science, often by interactive exhibits. Indeed, noting these changing priorities,

Hooper-Greenhill (1994: 1) has argued that 'the balance of power in museums is shifting from those who care for objects to include, and often prioritise, those who care for people'. However, to draw a distinction between organisations and institutions with the same objectives but different priorities is artificial and could be damaging.

Every object has a context, a history – a very individual story: it is that story that is the point of contact between the object and the museum visitor. Scientific artefacts only take meaning in context. Expert visitors, who may be scholars in a given field, 'bring the context with them'. They know what they want to look at, and indeed why they are looking at it. For the lay visitor the situation is very different. One of the Science Museum's unique strengths lies in the almost inexplicable but inherent human satisfaction of seeing the real thing – the *actual* Apollo command module that circled the moon; the *actual* Stephenson Rocket locomotive. But without an insight into the human endeavours of the pioneers of railways or the technology required for a human space mission, these artefacts become mere objects. It is the knowledge surrounding the objects that turns them into museum artefacts. Indeed, Stella Butler has argued (Butler, 1992: Chapter 6) that the significance of artefacts can be conveyed to visitors only if the items are located in particular cognitive frameworks which must themselves be shown to be indivisible from the societies in which they were formed. In order to address the needs of the non-expert a bridge is needed. It is the task of museum curators and exhibit designers to make that bridge, to contextualise the object and tell its personal story (see, for example, Velarde, 1992).

In museums and science centres, first-person interpretation has grown and developed alongside other communication strategies such as the provision of video-clips, tape–slide sequences, telephones, and all the other devices that seek to supply the story. Quin (1990: 197) noted the spread of 'interpreters' who bridge the gulf between the scientist/exhibit developer and the visitor. Many interpreters have been salaried, but with the current pressure on funding experienced by museums and science centres, it is unlikely that this type of activity can develop to meet visitors' needs and expectations without some imaginative enhancement of the process.

It is the thesis of this book, building upon and celebrating what has already been achieved, that professionals can amplify their impact by the selective and effective use of *volunteers* in the process of first-person interpretation.

1.3 Some aims and purposes of volunteering

More and more people are discovering the satisfaction of deploying their knowledge not only for economic gain but also for the sheer satisfaction to be had through the social contact and enhanced awareness that can flow from volunteer activity. This is a phenomenon to be welcomed and celebrated. In 1977, Fred Hirsch, in his seminal book *The Social Limits to Growth*, pointed not only to the folly of building our hopes on an ever-increasing exploitation of the world's physical resources but also to the folly of seeking so-called 'positional goods' – those that are enjoyed because of the social position they offer to those that have them compared to those that do not. Obvious examples are country cottages and motor cars. When everyone wants a country cottage, we end up with miles of suburbs; when everyone has a car, we all sit in traffic jams. Likewise, if we think of education as a positional good, we are going to have to constantly run faster in order to maintain 'position' as more and more people acquire education. He urges that education be seen as an end rather than as a means, to be enjoyed for the satisfaction of knowing rather than for any supposed economic advantage it may give. Volunteering to take part in the process of museum interpretation and/or in the many support activities in museums that build towards 'the museum experience' can give volunteers the type of satisfaction that represents sustainable social growth. Csikszentmihalyi and Hermanson (1996: 67) make a similar point: 'It would be difficult to see how a species as dependent on learning as we are could have survived if we did not find the process of making sense of our environment pleasurably rewarding.'

Who offers voluntary service and where does museum interpretation fit in? Hedley and Smith (1992) have surveyed the many forms of volunteer activity, which include: raising or handling money; serving on committees; organising or helping with events; secretarial or administrative work; providing transport; community service; representation or advocacy; and visiting people in institutions or counselling. Volunteering in the United Kingdom is, however, not yet spread evenly through society. Hedley and Smith (ibid.: 76–7) show that: women are slightly more likely to volunteer than men; the optimum age for volunteering is 35–44; there is a clear link between voluntary activity and socio-economic class, with the higher socio-economic groups showing the highest rates of participation; there is a link with education, in that those with university education were more likely to be volunteers than those with less education; volunteering is unevenly distributed throughout Britain (perhaps as a consequence of the link with social class), with the highest participation rates being found in the more prosperous South of England; people's propensity to volunteer increases with income – young, older, unemployed, and disabled people, and people from ethnic minorities, are underrepresented in formal volunteering. (The profile of volunteers in the USA is somewhat similar – see McCurley and Lynch, 1994: 2.) If we are to support the belief that volunteering is an end in itself, then opportunities to volunteer must be created not simply in response to gaps in service provision, but also in order to balance the needs of the end-user of the service (the museum visitor, the home-bound, infirm, etc.) with the personal needs of the individual volunteers (see Niyazi, 1996a, 1996b, 1996c, 1996d, 1996e). Museum volunteering provides a good example of how volunteering can meet the needs of both the volunteer service provider and the receiver of the service.

Within the museum world, volunteering has indeed been growing. In a survey for the Volunteer Centre (renamed in 1996 the National Centre for

Volunteering), sponsored by the Museums & Galleries Commission and with funds from the Office of Arts and Libraries, Mattingly (1984) found that volunteers were deployed in museums throughout the United Kingdom in the following activities: finds processing; excavation/fieldwork; conservation/ restoration; cataloguing and documentation (the largest area of activity); research; display/exhibition; sales/information; guiding/interpretation/adminis- tration/ funds/committees; and curatorial training. Some museums in her survey were run entirely by volunteers. Mattingly's (ibid.) profile of museum volunteers is somewhat similar to that offered by Hedley and Smith (1992), with the 18–30 and 31–60 age groups each constituting over one-third of the volunteers, while the under-18s and the over-60s between them constituted just over a quarter of the volunteers (Matlingly, 1984: 19); those with higher levels of education (post–18) being more heavily represented than those with lower levels (ibid.: 21); those in professional/managerial occupations being more highly represented than those from semi-skilled or unskilled occupations (ibid.: 22); and interest in the subjects dealt with in the museum being the overwhelming motivating factor (ibid.: 30).

Seven years later, introducing a publication of the Office of Arts and Libraries on Volunteers in Museums and Heritage Organisations, Millar could write:

> Volunteers are a significant part of the museum community. Volunteers are the ultimate frequent visitors. The growth of museums at the rate of one a fortnight in recent years is due mainly to the huge growth in voluntary trusts and 'all volunteer' museums. Yet, in the current debate on the function of museums in society the place of volunteers in museums merits scarcely a mention. It is important to redress the balance.
>
> (Millar, 1991: 1)

The present book is, in many ways, complementary to Millar's book, offering a description, with case studies, of projects in North America and the United Kingdom that translate into action ideas there adumbrated. Specifically, Millar's observation (ibid.: 20) that 'the status of guiding is changing from being considered a low level task to one of critical importance to the public profile of museums' is central to our argument.

In the United States, the role of docent is already well established (see Chapter Four). Many museums and galleries now employ someone specifically to organise the volunteer team, finding that to deploy volunteers to maximum effect, it is necessary to provide a well-organised system for recruitment, management and training. The organiser can be responsible for ensuring the best fit between volunteers and paid professionals. There is now a growing literature, to which the present volume is a UK contribution, on the effective management of volunteers – see, for example, Wilson (1976), Ellis (1986), Kuyper, Hirzy and Huftden (1993), McCurley and Lynch (1994).

1.4 Benefits and motivations in volunteering

What do volunteers gain from the service they render? This is a key question because all parties to a volunteering arrangement should expect to gain something from it. Reciprocity is required – efficient and effective service in exchange for some form of benefit. Today's volunteers do not, and in most cases cannot, work for 'nothing'. Apart from out-of-pocket expenses (and many volunteers do not ask for or receive these), volunteers need to receive in exchange for their gift of time something that serves their needs. What this 'gift' is will vary according to the volunteer. One example will indicate what is possible.

Students, who at present in the United Kingdom represent only 10 per cent of volunteers, represent a massive potential resource for museums. For the huge numbers of young people who have time, energy and enthusiasm to offer, the benefit of volunteering can come through *enhancement of their study*. Sometimes this enhancement comes from activities undertaken in parallel to their studies, with no explicit link being made between the study and the service. However, over the last 30 years, attempts have been made to bring these two elements of students' experience together. 'Study Service' is the term applied by the United Nations Educational, Scientific, and Cultural Organisation (UNESCO) to work in which students combine study leading towards the award of an academic qualification with some form of direct practical service to the community. (In the USA the equivalent term is 'Service Learning'.) Students undertaking Study Service do not compete with paid professionals; rather, they do work which could not otherwise have been done. In a major examination of Study Service in the United Kingdom (Whitley, 1980, 1982), Community Service Volunteers distinguished Study Service from staff consultancy/research on the one hand and from purely voluntary extracurricular student activities on the other. Four criteria distinguish Study Service from other work in which people in higher education serve society:

1 students (not staff alone) should be involved;
2 the work should be an integral part of the curriculum and preferably assessed;
3 there should normally be direct contact, at some stage of the course, between students and intended beneficiaries;
4 the effect of the work should be detectable at individual or small-group level.

In the United Kingdom, for example (see Goodlad, 1975, 1982), law students have given free legal advice to people who cannot afford professional fees; town planning students have helped tenants to formulate and express their views about planning proposals that might affect them; engineering students have studied the needs of the elderly and those on low incomes for systems and devices (telephones, meals-on-wheels, sheltered employment) that neither government nor private industry had examined; theology and sociology students have worked within a wide variety of community groups, statutory and voluntary, giving various sorts of practical service; students of languages have taught English to immigrants; and technical college students on day-release have built an adventure playground as part of their liberal studies. In every case, college staff have been involved to ensure that the service rendered is competent – the basic requirement of all community service; the use of community service as a focus for the students' learning has ensured reciprocity – both students and those whom they seek to serve benefiting in different ways. This diminishes the likelihood of paternalism on the one hand or exploitation on the other.

1.5 The Nuffield Science Interpretation Project

One variant of Study Service, tutoring by university students, has grown rapidly in recent years, not only in the United Kingdom and the USA but also in many other countries. Because the process of interpretation in museums is very similar to that of tutoring (in that both are attempts to assist people in 'locating' ideas and objects in meaningful frames of reference) and, like tutoring, is an ideal focus for Study Service, Chapter Three summarises some of the most important research on tutoring and highlights issues that will need to inform museum interpretation by volunteers. However, before we examine what volunteer interpreters can do, we must first 'locate' the role of volunteers within the range of possible purposes and functions of museums.

2

The functions of museums and the role of volunteers

Many of the functions of a museum are contradictory. This chapter discusses the aims and objectices of museums, and puts the role of volunteers into context.

Volunteers are both a potential resource and an audience. Volunteers can help museums to support their core aims by giving their time actively to assist with and contribute to the work that the museum does, or by raising money. Simultaneously volunteers are on the receiving end of many of the museum's services and are a significant and influential audience. For these reasons, the case for volunteers is here woven into a discussion on the basic functions of museums; we argue that the management of volunteers can be effective only if these functions are clearly understood, prioritised, and articulated.

Some issues raised here will be taken up in more detail in subsequent chapters. The North American case studies in Chapter Four provide examples of how five very different museums have each successfully integrated their volunteer programmes into their objectives and working practices. In Chapter 5, the pilot studies of volunteers in the Science Museum (London) illustrate both sustainable and unsustainable roles for volunteers. To contextualise this work, we refer to and in some cases review both literature and examples of volunteer deployment from both continents.

2.1 The functions of museums

Most museologists have remarked upon, or indeed explored, the different functions of a museum. The perspective that follows is by no means new, nor does it chart unexplored territory. It will, however, be particularly fruitful as a prelude to the study of the role of volunteers in museums.

Before a museum deploys volunteers it is essential to consider carefully the priorities of the museum and subsequently to manage volunteers to support those priorities. All of the less productive and even destructive activities of volunteers that have occurred can be explained by the museum not taking due care to consider:

- which areas of the museum could benefit from volunteer assistance;
- how volunteers could benefit from the opportunity of working in a museum;
- which methods should be used to ensure that the volunteers are managed and work effectively to support the museum's objectives, and gain from the experience.

In his seminal work *Museums in Motion*, published in 1907, Alexander (1979: 1) recognised that 'A museum is a complex institution and defining it is not easy'. More recently, Butler (1992: 1), reasserting this point, notes that most modern museums combine the care, preservation and study of valuable objects with the staging of exhibitions. 'They educate and also entertain. . . . Different museums place widely different emphasis on the various museum functions.'

A 'museum' can be almost all things to all people in the sense that a museum visit is a very personal combination of experiences. The case studies in Chapter Four illustrate this point. First, let us consider the material collection of objects that makes a museum. Wittlin (quoted by Chadwick, 1980) discusses the motivations for collecting, i.e., economic hoard collections, social prestige collections, magic collections, collections as expressions of group loyalty, collections as a means of stimulating curiosity and enquiry, collections as a means of stimulating or evoking emotional experience. This categorising of collections with regard to the motivation for collecting raises the issue of different museum priorities and objectives.

Most historical perspectives on museums make mention of what is believed to be the first ever museum – the Hellenistic museum of Alexandria (see, for example, Chadwick, 1980: 3 and Solinger, 1989: 1). Alexander (1990: 7) notes that the museum of Alexandria did have some objects but was chiefly a university or philosophical academy – 'a kind of institute of advanced study with many prominent scholars in residence and supported by the state'. When the Greeks used the word 'museum' (Greek *mouseion*), they referred primarily to a centre of learning.

The International Council of Museums (ICOM) defines a museum as:

> a non-profit making permanent institution in the service of society and of its development and open to the public which acquires, conserves, researches, communicates, and exhibits for the purposes of study, education and enjoyment, material evidence of man and his environment.
>
> (ICOM, 1990: 12)

This definition is all-encompassing and certainly complex. The question remains: What is a museum's key function? Out of all these activities, where should the emphasis lie? Can a museum practically or theoretically fulfil all these functions? The ICOM definition has gradually grown and developed, and even today there is considerable disagreement as to the relative importance of its various elements.

Using the ICOM definition as a focus for discussion we will consider three key issues:

1 Is it practically feasible for a museum to conserve and exhibit?
2 Can a museum exhibit for both enjoyment and education?
3 Is it, in fact, possible for a museum to simultaneously research and communicate all in the service of society and of its development?

It is very difficult for any organisation to have so many core functions. Certainly, the Audit Commission, in its report on managing local authority museums and art galleries in the United Kingdom, was aware of the tension:

> Within the Museum profession, parallel pursuit of the twin causes of conservation and exhibition creates tension. Achieving the right balance between stewardship and presenting the results of that to the public is not easy.
>
> (Audit Commission 1991: 6)

Lewis, in his brief world survey of museums, comments on an additional paradox: the public's perception of what museums are and the reality of what today's museums offer to the visitor.

> The classical associations of the term with the muses and contemplation, together with a strong tendency to collect, preserve and exhibit only high art and the exotic rather than a representative assemblage of our heritage has had a marked influence on the public perception of museums and their role in society.
>
> (Lewis 1984: 7)

By contrast, Lewis notes:

> However, the Museum today is in no sense maintaining a latter day classical tradition. Rather, at a general level, it seems to be a reflection of an inherent human propensity towards inquisitiveness and acquisitiveness combined with a wish to communicate to others; it also attempts to respond to present day social needs.
>
> (ibid.)

2.2 The inherent paradox of museums' functions

Exhibiting and conserving

> Within the museum profession, parallel pursuit of the twin causes of conservation and exhibition generates tension.
>
> (Audit Commission 1991: 6)

These two functions of a museum are, in fact, often in direct conflict. The ideal environment for an object to be stored for conservation purposes is generally in a dark, fairly cool, and stable environment – optimum humidity and temperature would depend upon the object's material and structure. For most purposes the ideal would be to store all objects in a closed dark environment far from the reach or sight of anyone. In reality, the most modern conservation stores do indeed store objects (in a highly inaccessible manner for the public) on racks similar to those of a warehouse. Such conditions certainly do not coincide with exhibiting.

Some museums try to get around this conflict of interests by exhibiting fragile or light-sensitive objects on a rolling programme or by making replicas of the original objects for display purposes only, while protecting and conserving the 'real' artefact. This latter option seems a good practical solution, funds permitting; but it poses two further problems: first, the essence of a museum depends on the 'real' object with its own special individual history, and second, the replica in itself becomes an artefact, as is the case with many of the working models built for the Science Museum (London) earlier this century.

Enjoyment and education

> The twentieth century has seen museums become less pompous and more egalitarian; they have continued to be for the public's benefit, largely through their educational work. During the last decade or so, however, museums have changed again. Their educational function has been reduced and they've become more concerned with entertainment, tourism and income generation.
>
> (Spalding, 1991: 63)

Can a museum be both enjoyable *and* educational? Spalding argues above that increasing entertainment value of museums has been at the cost of educational value (entertainment will be deemed in this context as synonymous with pleasure), thus implying that education and entertainment have an indirect relationship with one another. Many more specialists in informal learning believe that there is a false dichotomy of values between educational effectiveness and entertainment (see Bitgood, Serrel, and Thompson, 1994: 87). In Figure 2.1., a model presented by Friedman to the Ecsite conference 1995 (Friedman, 1995), it is argued that education and entertainment are directly proportional to one another. The actual mathematical function describing this proportionality is what most museum educationalists strive to realise.

Perhaps the word 'education' has too many connotations for the majority of writers to view it as being potentially synonymous with entertainment. Stephen Feber brings up this point in his essay entitled 'New approaches to science: in the museum or outwith the museum':

> Museums are increasingly being spoken of as institutions where informal learning takes place . . . I will use the word learning rather than education because the latter implies a programme of instruction, a syllabus and a certain formality and museums, after all, provide opportunities to learn but are not schools.
>
> (Feber, 1987: 85)

The leisure industry has come up with the idea of 'edutainment', emphasising

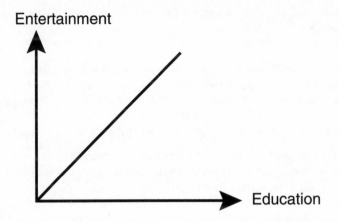

Entertainment

Education

Figure 2.1

that the two are by no means mutually exclusive. There is a growing body of research on the relationship between entertainment and education. Not surprisingly, with the public having increasing amounts of leisure time and disposable income (and perhaps a feeling that formal education is less than adequate), the leisure industries tend to support the theory that you can learn while being entertained.

These two functions of museums – education and entertainment – are of particular relevance for this study of museum volunteers for two reasons: first, the case studies indicate that, for the volunteers, education and entertainment are the dominant benefits, and second, because the volunteers' role is often to facilitate the visitors' learning, enjoyment and entertainment.

Research and communication

These two activities do not, by definition, conflict; in fact, they often depend on one another. In practice, however, one often has to be prioritised over the other. The research concerning specific objects is what causes us to recognise them as artefacts and turns storehouses into museums. Research and communication are dependent upon one another: without a 'potential audience' with whom to communicate, scholarly activity would be meaningless, and without research no principle of selection would emerge to suggest what was worth communicating and which objects were more valuable and interesting than others to collect, conserve and exhibit.

There are two main issues: first, the role of scholarly activity in the museum, and second, the purpose and ideals behind public access. Sir Neil Cossons, Director of the Science Museum (London), argues that there is no contradiction between popularisation and scholarship:

> The lifeblood of museums is their collections, the heartbeat is provided by good curatorship and conservation. The Museum if it is not a collection, is nothing. The common link between us all is the stuff of

13

museums. Scholarship will reveal its truths. But the customers for those collections and truths must have a voice too.

(Cossons, 1991: 24)

Peter Gathercole asks whether artefacts are regarded by curators as basic to the existence of museums, or whether it is rather the knowledge concerning artefacts that is basic, the artefacts being illustrative of that knowledge. He argues that museum artefacts are analogous to commodities in that they have properties bestowed upon them by virtue of their museum existence.

> They do not possess these properties intrinsic to themselves. The fetishism of artefacts, I suggest, exists when they are assumed to be what they are not. They are often regarded as evidence *per se* of cultural behaviour, but until this evidence is recognized, they remain, literally speaking, mere objects. Thus in Museum terms, the cultural status of artefacts, that is, the attribute which transfers objects into artefacts, depends upon the extent to which this attribute is perceived by curators, and is used by them in both research and display.
>
> (Gathercole, 1989: 74)

The reduction of public funding of museums often forces them to make a priority of short-term goals – increasing visitor numbers by satisfying the current 'audience' – over long-term objectives – investing money to develop and increase the museum's collections and knowledge about those collections for the future 'audience'. Therefore although the two activities of research and communication do not by definition conflict, it has been found in practice that research for future audiences has to be cut to satisfy the immediate demands of the current audience.

It cannot be overemphasised that a museum's mission is inevitably a compromise between conflicting interests. By definition, a museum is a place where one may muse; there will always be a debate over a museum's priorities and the conditions under which 'material evidence of man and his environment' are managed 'to serve society and its development'. Museums need not only to acknowledge that this internal conflict exists, but also to recognise the pressing need for museums to prioritise their many possible functions.

2.3 The ideals behind public access and community involvement

While not compromising the essence of what they are, museums have to increase their accessibility to the public. O'Neill (1991: 32) sees this as part of the challenge that faces all of the knowledge-based professions, namely that of opening themselves up, of becoming accessible so that there is a clear distinction between authority based on expertise and barriers based on group interest and exclusivity. This balance is a difficult one to maintain. It is physically impossible in the twentieth century to collect, conserve and communicate everything: even for mass communication, selections have to be made as to what to collect and who to inform. The heritage sector, by definition, acknowledges this as it supports a small elite who can develop and perpetuate our knowledge, and who train apprentices to take their work forward.

But how can such academic elitism marry with the modern imperative to communicate and interpret collections for the public? Washburn (1990: 200) reminds us that well into the nineteenth century access to European collections was limited to friends of the owner or carefully screened outsiders, and the form of the exhibit was of little significance. 'Those gaining access to the collections were by definition both qualified and anxious to profit from an examination of the objects however displayed.' To resolve the tension between seeing the museum *either* as a centre of academic excellence *or* as a public cultural centre, Washburn advocates separating casual visitors from serious students, with exhibits for the general public and research facilities for the qualified scholar (ibid.: 203).

It could be argued that many museums in the 1990s have already adopted such an approach, targeting exhibitions, visitor events and galleries at different audiences. Their varying needs are catered for with, for example, visual storage collections in public galleries which are a good way to provide easy access to parts of the collections previously on display only to the qualified scholar; improved documentation and records of collections on computer systems that can be accessed by the public increasingly through the Internet; improved exhibition design married with extensive visitor studies providing more eye-catching and accessible displays for the lay audience; raised standards of customer care providing an ever-improving service to the public and responding to all enquiries, however trivial they may seem.

The argument concerning accessibility has been going on for a long time; resistance to change has often stemmed from an old-established belief, the product of an aristocratic and hierarchical society, that art and scholarship are for a closed circle. As Grinder and McCoy (1985: 12) point out, in many American museums in the nineteenth century fees were charged 'for the purpose of keeping unacceptable visitors out'. In opposition to the view that high culture was for an educated elite, Dr Albert C. Barnes used his wealth, earned in the pharmaceutical industry, to build up a collection which he opened in 1922 for the benefit of working-class people. He believed passionately in the rights of all people to be educated, regardless of their race or socio-economic back-ground. And, indeed, he took this to extremes by allowing preferential access to the undereducated, often excluding rich aristocrats and businessmen whom he held in contempt for their treatment towards him as a self-made American millionaire. Barnes and a few other affluent collectors were ahead of their time in their belief that high culture can be both useful and enjoyable for society.

Bennet (1995: 19) argues that it was only in the mid to late nineteenth century that the relations between culture and government came to be thought of and organised in a distinctively modern way via the conception that the works, forms and institutions of high culture might become a government responsibility. He attributes to James Silk Buckingham the conception of culture's role in the practical agenda of reforming politics in early Victorian England.

There is a noticeable move towards increasing intellectual and physical accessibility to reach a broader section of the public. The (then) Department of National Heritage's support of a research study led by David Anderson and the subsequent report, *Museums and Learning in the UK* (Anderson, 1997), illustrates the move towards museums as an accessible learning resource. Anderson writes about 'an expanded concept of a Museum'. He discusses museum education as a collaborative process involving both public and staff, and the profound consequence of this is that education in museums lies not in what museums do *to* people with their objects, but rather in a process of individual and community development drawing upon the full range of community and institutional resources to which the public and the museum staff contribute as partners. He notes that those who fund museums are asking them to demonstrate that society as a whole is benefiting from the investment it makes (ibid.: Introduction).

There is an increasing number of exhibitions which cater specifically for local communities, with active involvement of local people in the planning of exhibitions. This idea of community involvement is illustrated in a number of the case studies in Chapter Four. In many of our activities – whether academic, leisure-based, religious – we are becoming increasingly aware of the benefits of multiculturalism. Simultaneously, most museums are also responding to the public's physical access requirements by providing bigger and better cafeteria facilities and quiet seating areas, and more toilets. As Bitgood, Serrel and Thompson note in a study of the impact of informal education on visitors to museums:

> This shift in process and attention to intended audience is not just an isolated unique occurrence for museums. A broader cultural shift underlies it: pluralism, systems and multiculturalism have become more important and fundamental philosophy has changed as well no single group is seen as having exclusive access to knowledge in the post modern mentality.
>
> (Bitgood, Serrel, and Thompson, 1994: 67)

2.4 A new function of museums and its implications: income generation

Roger (1987: 28), among others, has noted that every business – including museums – is under increasing pressure to justify its existence. 'Like it or not, museums are in competition with other forms of leisure, entertainment and educational activities.'

Building upon Friedman's graphical representation of the relationship between education and entertainment, another dimension can be added to the graph – money-making or income generation. Friedman, at the 1995 Ecsite conference, encouraged the delegates to think carefully about the growing competition and potential threat that theme parks and many other leisure industries are now posing. By marketing themselves as learning environments, such attractions are entering a market and targeting an audience that has previously been held by the heritage sector, museums and science centres. Disney World in Florida is even claiming to provide 'edutainment' through topiary classes. Learn how to make your hedge into a Mickey Mouse look-alike!

Exploring the implications of this new function of money-making, it is enlightening to consider briefly two other sectors of the leisure industry with which museums are finding themselves competing: corporate museums and theme parks. Corporate museums are one of the most frequently overlooked areas of the museum world. These museums and similar visitor centres are associated with manufacturing (see Danilov, 1991). They are operated by publicly owned trusts or privately held companies. Their functions are usually as public relations and/ or marketing exercises and sometimes simultaneously as convenient money-spinners – a kind of by-product for the manufacturing industry or corporation, e.g. Cadbury's World or the Sellafield Visitor Centre. The corporate museum movement had its beginnings in the nineteenth century when companies began to save examples of their products, long before they thought of creating museums or visitor centres. Hence the history of many corporate museums, like that of museums, was in the collection of objects. The primary difference between corporate museums and other museums and science centres discussed so far lies, perhaps, not in the objectives of the museum or visitor centre (which may indeed include education and entertainment and be based around a collection), but in the principal objectives of its supporting funders – to make money – and the power and influence that these principal objectives have on the priorities of corporate museums or visitor centres.

Theme parks are another comparable sector of the leisure industry. These sometimes overlap with corporate museums – Legoland in Windsor being a case in point. The primary function of a theme park is to make money. Unlike corporate museums, they are self-funding and therefore, by definition, their priority is income generation.

The additional axis added to Friedman's diagram (see Figure 2. 2.) illustrates the various competing functions of three divisions of the leisure industry

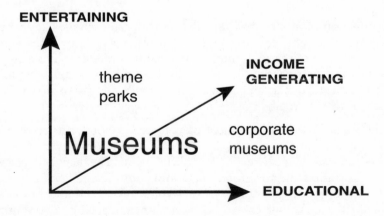

Figure 2.2

discussed above – museums and science centres, theme parks, and corporate museums. It can be argued that corporate museums, as by-products of a productive money-making company, are more defined by their educational function than by their entertainment function – in so far as their funding may not be dependent on the number of visitors.

Some theme parks, leisure centres and corporate museums could possibly be included under the umbrella term 'museum' as defined by ICOM. Most museums and science centres in the 1990s have had to incorporate many of the functions of theme parks and corporate museums, and theme parks and corporate museums now fulfil many of the functions that define museums. It is often only their priorities and core values that differ.

The importance of assigning institutional objectives and priorities

Rather than trying to define museums and non-museums too rigidly, the above discussion sought to raise awareness of the possibly conflicting functions of a museum. The aim was to give an overview of the breadth of a museum's activities, and to give a picture of the encroaching roles of other business activities on territory previously held primarily by museums. The issues raised are intended to encourage museum employees to think creatively about what makes their museum's priorities and objectives unique.

> The priorities assigned to the different museum functions are important in establishing the essence of any museum, and its board of trustees, director, curators, educational staff, conservators, designers, and other specialists should ponder its basic purposes as well as try to find ever more effective ways of achieving them.
>
> (Alexander, 1979: 15)

2.5 The unique support available to non-profit income-generating museums: sponsorship, corporate events, membership, and volunteers

The new function of money-making has meant that museums, like many other publicly funded cultural centres, have had to reconsider how they can effectively position themselves to command the public's interests. Enticing visitors through the doors is essential for a museum's continued existence, numbers of visitors equating to direct support gained through admission fees or indirect support through the credibility of a museum as a worthy cause.

We would argue that the deployment of volunteers should not be seen simply as an extension of personnel service. The administration may be comparable and indeed shared, but there are key differences. The benefits received by volunteers are different; therefore, the motivations behind volunteering are different; therefore, the types of work that volunteers could and would sustain are often different. Volunteers are as much an audience as a resource and, we argue, should be managed in a comparable way to sponsors or members.

Sponsorship managers have to find the right sponsor for the right gallery, project, etc., and maintaining a sponsor is not an easy task. As with volunteers, sponsors often want to gain something, albeit it something intangible, from the arrangement. Membership managers have to keep the members informed of all the developments in the museum and explain how the museum can serve their needs. Managers of volunteers would gain from looking at the particular relationships that the museum has with members and sponsors and incorporate the methods used to manage and serve members and sponsors into their volunteer management style.

The risks associated with museum volunteers often overshadow the benefits because many museum staff cannot think beyond the idea that volunteers are simply an extension of the paid staff. We argue in this study that volunteers are more than simply unpaid staff. While acknowledging the risk of volunteers supplanting paid staff, and indeed of volunteers being exploited as unpaid labour, employing paid staff or indeed any other museum activity has its associated risks. The difference with volunteers is that these risks are often not identified and therefore not managed (Tremper and Kostin, 1993). It is unfortunate that volunteer management has often lacked any such risk assessment and the huge and unique benefits that volunteers can bring to a museum (as advocates, fundraisers, unpaid staff members, etc., providing added value and a link to the community – see Ellis, 1986), are overlooked. As a consequence, museum volunteers have received a bad press when in fact it is more than likely to be museum staff and managers who are at fault.

In a recent interview, Christopher Bland, Chairman of the British Broadcasting Corporation (BBC), indicated that there are many other organisations dependent upon local and central government funding that are having to question their previous functions and the way in which they are managed. Bland defined public service broadcasting as

> broadcasting driven by non-commercial objectives. Its objectives must be to do the best possible job within the non-commercial criteria of the media it is in – to produce the best possible range and quality of programming in television or radio that you can produce with the resources that you are given by the licence fee payer.
>
> (Gordon, 1996: 62)

The BBC is in a position comparable to that of a modern museum. It has to be accountable to its funders – or at least those who have the authority to ensure its continued funding. When Bland was asked 'Should the BBC compete by trying to do the same thing – except more and better or should it compete by offering something different to do both?' his reply was:

> You can't do both. Either you are going to take the competition head on and here is where we are going to find resources to do it – this is how we are going to match the exponentially rising costs of sporting events and films or you say we are not going to take them head on; we don't have the resources to do it and we will do something different.

19

Museums, likewise, will have to 'do something different' if they are to adapt to today's changing circumstances. Our thesis is that museum interpretation by volunteers will be that 'something'. Before indicating how it can best be organised, we will review, in Chapter Three, some of the research on student tutoring which seeks to meet similar objectives and which has important messages for museum interpretation.

3

The development of student tutoring as a form of volunteering

For museum interpretation to flourish and expand, we believe that it will become increasingly necessary for museum professionals to delegate some of their work to non-professionals. Specifically, much of the day-to-day business of explaining could be delegated to volunteers. The Nuffield Science Interpretation Project (described in Chapter Five) drew inspiration from the confirmed success over many years of student tutoring as a form of volunteering. As the present chapter will argue, students who act as tutors to other young people have much to gain from the activity – and the instruction that they can offer can be of high quality. Although most of this book concentrates on issues of management, it is useful to review the benefits that can flow from tutoring – itself a form of interpreting.

Student tutoring has a long and distinguished history, and as a process of instruction has been thoroughly researched (see Appendix A). In modern usage, student tutoring involves students from colleges and universities helping pupils in local schools on a sustained and systematic basis under the direction and supervision of teachers (Goodlad, 1995a: 2). The students do not replace the teachers; rather, they amplify their effects. Currently, some 200,000 young people world-wide are receiving tutoring from college students through schemes modelled on the Pimlico Connection, a student tutoring scheme developed at the Imperial College of Science, Technology and Medicine, University of London. Because the scheme has been thoroughly researched over a period of 20 years and the findings are highly relevant to the comparable field of museum interpretation, it is described briefly here.

3.1 The Pimlico Connection model

Student tutoring began at Imperial College in 1975 with a pilot project funded by the Leverhulme Trust. The principal object of this project was to see if the presence of student tutors could make science, mathematics, and (what was then called) craft design technology (CDT) more enjoyable for school pupils, and to simultaneously provide students with a challenging way of improving their skills in the communication of scientific ideas.

In the academic year 1975/6, 12 electrical engineering students visited the Pimlico School weekly for 15 weeks to help with the teaching of Combined Science to third-year classes. In a deliberate invocation of the titles of two films, *Passport to Pimlico* and *The French Connection*, the scheme was called the Pimlico Connection. The students carried out an evaluation of the tutoring as their third-year socio-technical group project (Abidi *et al.*, 1976). In 1976/7, a second group of students carried out another group project to evaluate a more complex scheme involving 19 students deployed in various combinations (Anslow *et al.*, 1977). In 1977/8, 34 students acted as tutors (Goodlad, Atkins, and Harris, 1978). In subsequent years, the tutoring was extended to other schools, including primary schools, and patterns discernible in the early research data became clearer and stronger (Goodlad, 1985).

Research on the Pimlico Connection revealed that, over the first 12 years of its life, significant numbers of student tutors had been attracted into teaching as a career. In the light of this information, the (then) University Grants Committee (UGC) of the United Kingdom provided Dr Sinclair Goodlad in 1987 with a two-year grant to disseminate information about the Imperial College scheme. The project was one of a number to improve the flow into teaching of graduates in science, engineering and mathematics. (The UGC funded at the same time three other projects in the United Kingdom based upon the Pimlico Connection – at Cambridge, East Anglia and Warwick Universities.) The centrepiece of the project was an international conference on peer tutoring held at Imperial College in April 1989. A pre-conference book was published – Goodlad and Hirst (1989) – and a book of proceedings was published afterwards – Goodlad and Hirst (1990).

In 1990, a new project commenced at Imperial College, funded by British Petroleum's 'Aiming for a College Education' programme, to which Mr J. C. Hughes was appointed as the BP Fellow for Student Tutoring. The use of student tutors was thought to provide positive role models to children who might never have heard of a university, let alone thought of studying at one. The aims of the BP-funded project were threefold: first, to run and expand the Pimlico Connection at Imperial College; second, to promote the growth of similar schemes across the United Kingdom; and third, to undertake research on the possible effects of student tutoring in raising the aspirations of young people who were tutored.

In a parallel project, through the good offices of Sir Brian Jenkins, the then Lord Mayor of London and one of the trustees of Community Service Volunteers (CSV), CSV obtained support from industry and commerce (notably British Petroleum, British Telecom, National Power, the National Westminster Bank and Royal Mail), to promote tutoring schemes nation-wide under the heading 'Learning Together' (CSV, 1995a, 1995b; Potter, 1995).

With BP's help, the number of students acting as tutors in the Pimlico Connection expanded to its current annual number of 150. Through collaboration between the BP–Imperial College project and CSV's 'Learning Together', the number of schemes modelled on the Pimlico Connection increased from five in 1990 to 180 in 1995. Research on the third aim is still in progress. Through the BP International Mentoring and Tutoring Project, student tutoring is also being developed in other parts of the world. Representatives from 34 countries attended an international conference on the subject in London in 1995 (see Goodlad, 1995a). Similar world-wide interest was shown in a follow-up conference in April 1997.

Early in the life of the Pimlico Connection, students accompanied the pupils who received tutoring (tutees) on visits to the Science Museum (London); but it was not until 1992/3 that a pilot programme was developed to deploy student tutors as interpreters there. This project, and its sequels, are described in detail in Chapter Five.

3.2 Evaluation: benefits of tutoring – to teachers, tutors and school pupils

The benefits to participants in tutoring schemes are now well-documented (Goodlad, 1979; Goodlad and Hirst, 1989, 1990; Topping, 1988). Some findings regarding the Pimlico Connection are instructive. In the early years of the scheme, qualitative comments were solicited from selected participants (teachers, students, and pupils) through interviews, and from all participants through open-ended questionnaires that used sentence stubs to stimulate responses ('The best thing about having tutors in my class was . . . ', 'Tutoring would have been better if . . . ', etc.). In subsequent years, questionnaires were administered to teachers, student tutors, and the tutees incorporating statements drawn from the early qualitative studies. The *17th Annual Report of the Pimlico Connection* (Hughes, 1992) records the cumulative total of questionnaires given over a number of years to 918 student tutors, 8,309 pupils and 301 teachers. The findings, which are strikingly similar to findings regarding similar schemes elsewhere in the United Kingdom (e.g. Beardon, 1990; Green and Hughes, 1992; Hector Taylor, 1992), show the following:

Student tutors (replies *n* = 633/918: response rate = 69 per cent) report that they achieve:

- good practice in communicating scientific ideas (95 per cent);
- increased self-confidence (76 per cent);
- reinforcement of knowledge of their own subjects (59 per cent);
- an opportunity to get to know people with a different social background (81 per cent);
- the feeling of doing something useful (92 per cent).

School pupils (replies *n* = 5,629/8,309: response rate = 68 per cent) report that with student tutors lessons are:

- more interesting (55 per cent);

- easier to follow (63 per cent);
- more enjoyable (54 per cent).

Also, 54 per cent reported that they thought they learned more with tutors present.

Teachers in whose classes student tutors worked (replies *n* = 186/301: response rate = 62 per cent) report that with tutors:

- lessons were easier to handle (63 per cent);
- teaching was more enjoyable (70 per cent);
- pupils seemed to learn more than usual (69 per cent).

Throughout its life, the Pimlico Connection has concentrated on science, technology, and mathematics. It is reassuring, therefore, that research shows that similar effects occur for students tutoring in a wide range of subjects. In a report on research on 853 tutors working in the 'Learning Together' schemes sponsored by CSV, Hill and Topping (1995) note that the following cognitive skills seem to be enhanced by being a tutor:

- understanding of others' learning;
- communication of facts;
- practical demonstration;
- applying knowledge in new situations.

The majority of tutors also reported gains in the following transferable skills:

- oral communication;
- listening and questioning.

Interestingly, despite positive comments from teachers, research on the effect of being tutored on pupils' aspirations towards higher education was inconclusive (which is typical of attitudinal research) in one major study in Birmingham, although teachers spoke warmly of the influence on the student tutors on their pupils' aspirations towards higher education, there was no striking difference in this regard between tutored pupils and controls (Campbell, 1995). The researcher suggests two possible reasons for this: first, that white, female, middle-class tutors may not have been appropriate role models for ethnic minority pupils in an inner city area, and second, that not enough time was provided in the tutoring arrangements for the students to pass on information about university (ibid.: 165).

In the USA, in a project specifically involving science interpretation in a 'museum', similar results to those for the Pimlico Connection were found by Diamond *et al.* (1987) in their study of the long-term impact on teenagers of teaching science to the public in the San Francisco Exploratorium's Explainer Programme. From 50 to 80 per cent of 116 explainers studied mentioned that the programme had had a major impact on them with respect to: ability to teach people (80 per cent); desire to work with people (73 per cent); desire to learn on your own (63 per cent); understanding of your capabilities (62 per cent); self-confidence (60 per cent); and effectiveness in other jobs (50 per cent).

3.3 What lessons does student tutoring suggest for museum interpretation by volunteers?

Most of the lessons from the experience of tutoring will seem to be self-evident truths; they have, however, been learned from numerous schemes, often by painful experience. The observations that follow shaped our study (reported in Chapter Five) of museum interpretation projects by volunteers. Many of the points here examined are re-examined in Chapter Six, with detailed reference to museum practice. The points that follow draw upon Goodlad and Hirst (1989: Chapter Seven).

Define aims

As in the analysis of any form of communication, the key question is: Who is to communicate what to whom for what purpose?

Although the benefits of a tutoring arrangement may seem self-evident to all concerned, it is valuable for the organiser of a scheme to write down the specific objectives. For example: Are the benefits sought primarily academic/intellectual or social? If a compromise has to be made, as it often has to be, between benefits accruing to tutors and those accruing to tutees, in whose favour will the scheme operate? Likewise, the organisation of a scheme, the selection of participants, the choice of tutoring materials, etc. all depend upon the scheme's objectives.

Klaus (1975) stresses that it is important not to attempt too much. To maintain the morale of all concerned, the objectives of a tutoring scheme should be simple and readily achievable so that everyone may see how the scheme is working. The clarity and thrust of a tutoring scheme is best served if its objectives can be stated in a single sentence. For example: 'To give 15-year-old pupils detailed assistance with GCSE mathematics by providing university students as tutors.'

The implication of the above for museum interpretation work could be that closely targeted interventions with volunteers (possibly linked to special projects) may be more satisfactory than loose assignments to collections.

Structure the content

For the organiser of a tutoring scheme, a major decision is the degree of control to exercise over the content of the teaching. The two extreme conditions are (a) when tutors are given complete responsibility for choosing materials, and (b) when tutors operate with programmed texts in which steps are laid down very precisely.

It has long been known that striking benefits to tutees can come from the administration by tutors of programmed material (see, for example, Ellson *et al.*, 1965; Ellson, Harris, and Barber, 1968; Ellson, Barber, and Harris, 1969; Harrison, 1969, 1971a, 1971b, 1972a, 1972b; Ellson and Harris, 1970; Ellson, 1986). Not only does careful structuring ensure that learners are given material in an appropriate sequence, but it has also been found that tutors still find the human interaction rewarding. Tutors' originality and creativity can be built around the content whose structure is the prime responsibility of the trained teacher. Tutors, in short, do not re-invent the wheel; rather they use other people's wheels to travel further and faster.

The implication for museum interpretation is that the aims of an interpretation project can and should be translated into precise and specific tasks for the volunteers, but with opportunities for the volunteers to weave in their own ideas and suggestions.

Define roles and logistics

When tutoring schemes have failed, two major factors have often been present: (a) a lack of communication – people who should have known what was going on and did not; and/or (b) a loss of initiative and impetus – nobody seemed to know who was responsible for what. Most of these difficulties can be circumvented if one single person is given overall responsibility for a project.

Communication and logistics are without doubt the most difficult aspects of tutoring. Education has become so specialised and fragmented that frequently teachers in schools and colleges do not know what other teachers are doing. Indeed, conventional classroom teaching is often a very lonely and private activity. By contrast, peer tutoring, which frequently involves interactions between at least two groups of people, requires movement across many boundaries – some of which are defended with fierce intellectual territoriality.

There is no formula to achieve effective communication, although for those who like a systems approach, Melaragno (1976) offers a step-by-step approach for introducing peer tutoring. Communication is, however, greatly facilitated if the co-ordinator of a tutoring scheme produces a brief 'statement of intent', a document defining the aims of the scheme and describing briefly the procedures of administration and evaluation involved. Likewise, an annual report on a scheme (or a series of reports on mini-schemes) can be very useful, not only as a permanent record for participants (student tutors in particular value this), but also as material to offer to people coming into the scheme for the first time.

Because the negotiation of the roles of volunteers in museums is so complex, the focus of the Nuffield-funded project on which this book is based was on the management of volunteers.

Get secure finance

The history of student tutoring is littered with schemes that came to life with injections of trust fund or foundation money but which withered away when the initial period of funded work ended. It is for this reason that tutoring as a form of study service is attractive. If the tutoring is integrated with the students' studies, the cost of administering the activity becomes a legitimate charge upon the teaching establishment.

What has sometimes been forgotten is that while the services of volunteers are often freely given, there are necessary costs involved in maintaining a scheme – notably that of the full employment costs (salary, pension scheme, National Insurance) of the professional organiser of a scheme. Translated to the museum field, the issue of finance has several important aspects that are addressed in section 6.4. While it may seem attractive to deploy volunteers only on special projects for which earmarked funding is obtained, the lesson from tutoring is that, for a modest investment of 'core' funding, an organisation can release significant amounts of volunteers' time to which a notional value can readily be assigned.

Train the tutors/mentors

Not surprisingly, it has been known for many years that untrained tutors are less effective than trained ones (see, for example, Niedermeyer, 1970; Conrad, 1975); evidence about this continues to be produced (see, for example, Fuchs *et al.*, 1994; Shore, 1995). Topics usually covered in training sessions for tutors include: how to start a session by establishing a friendly atmosphere; familiarity with the content of the syllabus; what to do when a tutee gives a correct answer; what to do when a tutee is wrong; what to do if a tutoring session goes badly; how to vary the content of tutoring sessions; how to end a session; and how to keep records.

Training volunteers has been found to be one of the most rewarding aspects of tutoring because the professional person can use his or her knowledge to best effect. Also, just as the very process of tutoring can help tutors to organise their thoughts, so the planning of training can help professionals to organise theirs. In the university world, the linkage between teaching and research is not just to ensure that teaching is informed by the fruits of research, it is also to provide repeated opportunities for university teachers to reflect upon the aims, purposes and foundations of their disciplines.

It is through the training of volunteers that museum personnel can enjoy first-hand interaction with volunteers, and the volunteer organiser can maintain fruitful contact with colleagues. This important matter is addressed in section 6.5.

Support the tutors/mentors

In a tutoring scheme, the professional teacher passes on to non-professionals responsibility for tactics while maintaining tight control on strategy. Indeed, one of the most attractive features of tutoring is precisely this. As the pioneer Joseph Lancaster wrote: 'it is disgusting to teachers of any description to be continually plodding over the same ground of elementary arithmetic. Sameness, in every instance, produces listlessness; and variety is ever productive of agreeable sensations' (Salmon, 1932: 18). If teaching materials are properly organised, it should not, in theory, be necessary for a highly trained person to administer them.

> Any boy of 8 years old, who can barely read writing, and numerate well, is, by means of the guide containing sums, and the key thereto,

> qualified to teach the first four rules of arithmetic, simple and compound, if the key is correct, with as much accuracy as mathematicians who may have kept school for 20 years.
>
> (ibid.: 21)

The professional teacher ensures a proper interrelationship between strategy and tactics not only in the ways already specified (defining aims, structuring the content, ensuring proper consultation and defining roles, and training the tutors), but also in providing detailed support for the tutors. Ideally, this support will include regular debriefing sessions which can form part of the study of a study service arrangement. If that is not possible (and even when it is), the teaching materials need to have built-in instructions to keep the tutors on the right lines. Social gatherings have also been found to be desirable to oil the wheels of a system.

In the museum context, good written materials for volunteers (pointing up aspects of exhibits to explain) will be needed, as well as social gatherings at which to show that volunteers are valued. In section 6.6, other modes of support suitable for the museum context are examined.

Evaluate the scheme

Apart from the possibility that a contribution may be made to our collective understanding of the factors that make for success or failure in tutoring schemes, there are two major reasons for undertaking some sort of evaluation of schemes. First, one's perception of suitable objects for a scheme is sharpened if one tries to determine how one will know if those objects have been achieved. Second, everyone involved in a scheme (tutors and tutees, as well as administrators) will feel satisfaction if there is 'something to show for it all'. Just as a 'statement of intent' can sharpen perceptions, so an evaluative report can serve as a useful instrument with which to 'pass on the baton' and maintain continuity from one year to the next.

At the crudest level, evaluation can consist of anecdotal observations about a scheme from all participants. A more systematic approach is to generate simple rating scales (based on the substance of free responses in previous years) inviting reactions to specific aspects of a scheme. To give 'consumers' of a product a chance to offer their views, even if only by spending a minute checking a few boxes, puts out important signals about how seriously they are taken by 'management'.

Section 6.7 examines how museum interpretation by volunteers can be assisted by suitable evaluation.

3.4 Concluding observations

The research on student tutoring has two important messages for the further development of museum interpretation by volunteers. First, not only can volunteers make significant contributions to the process of communication, but they can also benefit from doing so in many and various ways. Second, although the fundamental process of communication is simple, the organisation of the conditions in which it can take place is not. The efforts of volunteers can be put to best effect if properly organised by a professional in the field. In short, in any scheme there has to be one person with whom the buck stops.

4

Case studies of five exemplary programmes in Canada and the USA

The object of this chapter is to describe in a qualitative manner five North American volunteer programmes that have made effective use of volunteers, and which exemplify the art of adapting the standard recommended management practices and procedures to attain and meet particular organisational missions and core objectives. It does not seek to be either comprehensive or definitive. Chapter Five describes projects in the Science Museum (London) that seek to draw upon the principles of good practice evolved both in the tutoring schemes described in Chapter Three and in the projects described in this chapter. Chapter Six analyses factors that seem particularly important in sustaining schemes.

Examples are drawn from Canada and the USA primarily because the deployment of volunteers as interpreters is more in evidence in museums there than in the United Kingdom; volunteer management is recognised as a distinct and special skill; and the deployment of volunteers is systematically incorporated into museums' missions and activities.

At the beginning of our research into volunteer programmes, exemplary British case studies were sought. Thirty of the 120 museums listing themselves under the heading 'Science and Industry' in the Reed Information Service (Valentine, 1994) were contacted. Of these 30, 80 per cent said that volunteers were deployed in some capacity; 90 per cent of these described their activities as limited, i.e., just in the café, only at special events, just behind the scenes, only with certain more flexible members of staff, etc.

There is already much good practice in the United Kingdom with a rich variety of volunteer management structures and volunteer roles. We mention just three. The first is a small independent museum, the Scottish Fisheries Museum in Fife, which is run predominantly by volunteers. There are 10 full-time and part-time staff, and 60–70 volunteers. Most of the volunteers have retired from the fishing industry. The museum is 25 years old and the volunteer role has expanded and developed as volunteers have offered their services. The museum has an impressively flexible pragmatic approach to the role of their volunteers and paid staff.

Second, the Museum of Transport, Manchester, is an independent museum run solely by its members: there are no paid staff. Some members, the subscribers, simply receive the journal; the other 30 members come in and work. Many of the members are private owners of the museum objects; they usually pay rent for the storage of their objects. The museum has developed professional policies and practices, and it is a pleasure to visit and see the entire staff having a sense of ownership and a real stake in the museum.

A third example of good practice (in the provision of a network of local authority and city museums) is in Scotland where the Glasgow Art Gallery and Museums Association (GAGMA) helps Glasgow museums by providing the free services of volunteer guides and contributing to the purchase of items for the collections. New guides are trained by experienced guides. A great deal of emphasis is put on the volunteer's individual efforts and motivation to learn.

Many UK museums now have friends' organisations that supply voluntary services, and some major organisations, such as the National Trust, have deployed volunteers as interpreters. Volunteers were working in museums, particularly those started by local learned societies, long before friends organisations came onto the scene, and a great many small independent museums depend entirely on voluntary staff (see Heaton, 1992). However, the examples from North America that we have chosen (and which were all visited) illustrate procedures we would particularly wish to commend.

The argument for strategic volunteer management

Eckstein (1992: 48) notes that the larger national museums are multi-million-pound enterprises and suggests that this fact strengthens the argument for a sound business approach to their operations over and above the primary concerns of curatorship and scholarship. He also reminds us that museums are labour-intensive: in all the national museums in the United Kingdom, staff costs account for the largest single area of expenditure. It is in supplementing and complementing the work of paid staff that volunteering is likely to have its biggest impact.

In North America, a directory of museum volunteer programmes (Nielsen, 1988), which includes entries from over 700 museums, illustrates:

- the recognition of volunteers' contribution to museums;
- the effective integration of volunteers in management procedures;
- extensive planning and networking skills in this field.

The American Association of Museum Volunteers (AAMV) that publishes this directory was founded in 1979. It is recognised by and affiliated nationally with the American Association of Museums (AAM) and internationally with the World Federation of Friends of Museums (WFFM). The AAMV is the organisation representing volunteers in American museums. One of its key purposes is to provide a means of communication between those involved with volunteer programmes.

What the programmes reported below have taught us is that there are crucial questions that need to be asked before, during and after the development of a volunteer programme for it to be a continuing success. The answers to these questions, which are explored in a discursive mode in this chapter and as a more analytical checklist in Chapter Six, provide readers with a *form* for a volunteer programme but not a *formula*. The case studies that follow are of organisations with, in our judgement, outstanding strengths in their approach to the use of volunteers. Each includes extracts from the mission statement of the museum, and a brief description of it in its specific location and community.

4.1 The Oakland Museum of California, USA: careful training of volunteers and the provision of written support materials

> The Oakland Museum of California offers visitors the opportunity to experience the full scope of California's ecology, history and art gathered together in one memorable place.
>
> (Oakland Museum of California, 1994b)

The Oakland Museum of California, opened in 1969, is a regional museum that brings together in one place the energies and disciplines of three earlier Oakland museums: the Oakland Public Museum (founded 1910) which was dedicated primarily to American Indian ethnological and American historical displays; the Oakland Art Museum (founded 1916); and the Snow Museum of Natural History (founded 1922). The museum tells the story of California in three areas: art, history, and natural sciences. Permanent collections and exhibits in the three main galleries are augmented by special exhibits, displays, lectures, films, seminars and other activities.

The museum is a municipally owned and operated institution with an operating budget of $9 million. As a department of the City of Oakland it receives $5 million of its annual budget from the city for all salaries and maintenance of the building. The remaining $4.2 million is self-engendered, provided through the generous support of the 9,000 museum members and donors, corporations, foundations, and state and federal funding agencies. Annual attendance is about 350,000 including 70,000 schoolchildren.

The staff efforts are enhanced by the work of over 1,300 dedicated volunteers. Volunteers support the museum in many ways and in many places: as docents, in offices, at the information desks and in the restaurant. The position of docent attracts the majority of volunteers. The word 'docent' is not generally used in the United Kingdom (it is not, for example, listed in the *Concise Oxford Dictionary*). It is used in many different contexts in North America. A definition is therefore needed. *Webster's* dictionary defines a docent as 'a lecturer or teacher'. The Oakland Museum of California's description is more useful:

> In the museum experience the docent role is not only to inform but to enlighten, not only to teach but to guide visitors of all ages in the

explorations of the exhibits in relation to their past experiences and understanding.

(Oakland Museum of California, 1994a: 1)

Prior to the opening of the Oakland Museum of California in September 1969, it became apparent that volunteer assistance would be needed to provide interpretative tours. Training classes were formed under the direction of the art, history and natural sciences curatorial staffs. In 1969, the Docent Council was formed to co-ordinate the activities of the three docent groups and to provide a vehicle for joint programming and future recruitment. Since the museum opened, the Docent Council has achieved national recognition and played an important role in assisting the museum to meet the recreational and cultural needs of its community and the museum's many visitors from throughout its region, the country and the world (cf., ibid.)

Our first tentative enquiry to the museum requesting assistance with the research for this book resulted in the arrival of a bulging envelope providing comprehensive documentation on the volunteers' activities: daily staff rosters, copies of recent docent field-trip invitations, the *Schools Program Guide*, and training manuals for their volunteer teams. The innovative programme of the Oakland Museum of California has impressed and enthused many other museum staff and volunteers, and disseminating their skills and expertise is now one of the museum's key activities. A national docent symposium, 'Extending Connections', was run by the museum in 1985 which brought over 400 docents and museum educators to Oakland for three days. From the symposium, a handbook of touring techniques was published. The introduction to this handbook provides an excellent insight into the museum's philosophy emphasising the importance of first-person interpretation:

> Museums do not simply teach, they communicate. The impulse toward communication and learning can be seen in the exhibitions, which involve the display of objects on view; brochures and catalogues which can tell a more complete story; interpretative programmes which provide a context for looking and obtaining new information; and guided tours by docents, which present concepts and facts to the public. Museums communicate with everyone as the knowledge and personal experience visitors bring to looking at objects varies not only with age but also with the number of times they have looked at the collection.
>
> (Oakland Museum of California, 1985: 1)

The Oakland Museum Docent Council produces a leaflet for docents, 'You Grow, We Grow', which gives a clear picture of what is offered to, and what is expected from, docents:

WELCOME TO THE WORLD OF TOURING
The Oakland Museum of California offers you unlimited volunteer opportunities. As a docent you work with diverse audiences, changing exhibitions, administration of the docent programme, tour development and community programmes.

WHAT WE GIVE
Docents at the Oakland Museum of California receive professional
training, continuing education, and year round programmes that educate
and invigorate

- monthly lectures on stimulating topics
- continuing education from museum professionals
- field trips to galleries, historic places and ecological sites
- symposia, conferences, and book reviews

HOW YOU QUALIFY
Your in-depth training for conducting interpretative tours of museum
exhibits involves participation in a programme consisting of academic
work, gallery training, field trips, independent study and research. There
is a fee for this training. [The fee is currently $100.]

WHAT DO YOU GET
Many varied opportunities await you as a docent. As well as leading
tours of the permanent collections and attending interesting monthly
programmes, you may also conduct tours featuring highlights of the
Museum, Indian Life and the Gold Rush. Other options are tours for
seniors which conclude with afternoon tea in the museum restaurant and
tours for the deaf and hearing impaired which are given by specially
trained docents.

(Oakland Museum Docent Council, 1994)

The docent is seen as a paraprofessional who serves the museum by giving
interpretative tours to scheduled school and adult groups, as well as individual
visitors, thus fulfilling an important public relations role for the Oakland
Museum of California. Tours last between one and one and a half hours, sometimes ending in an activity. The annual schools event brochure, a glossy A4
booklet of 20 pages, advertises and details all the schools events on offer to
teachers to enrich their classroom study. School pupils develop their visual and
enquiry skills as trained volunteer docents guide them in exploring museum
objects and exhibits.

More than 400 Oakland Museum of California docents provide interpretative
tours to some 60,000 people each year, enriching volunteers and visitors
alike. The provision of such a diverse programme of tours to schoolchildren
and adults requires college-level training, and demands cohesive management
practices. These are provided by the Docent Council.

The Docent Council is a fellowship of volunteers whose primary purpose is
to provide skilled interpretation of Californian art, history, and ecology,
to develop awareness of the interrelationships between individuals and their
environment, and to strengthen the educational offerings of the museum.
To become a member of the Docent Council, a volunteer must be a docent
who has completed training. The Docent Council programme, which is
self-administered, presents volunteers with many opportunities to serve in
leadership roles.

At the very heart of the museum is the Docent Centre – arranged around a large lounge-cum-study-cum-library with connecting doors. There is an inviting reading/meeting table in the main room and low bookshelves lining the walls. There are noticeboards tidily covered in formal and informal memos and news. This is officially a meeting place and the administrative centre for docents. Office space for the Docent Council staff leads off the central room. It is a learning centre for anyone who wants to learn and can make a regular time commitment to the museum.

The volunteers' commitment is astounding. All have taken college-level courses in their chosen discipline, on-gallery training under the direction of the curatorial staff and tour-techniques training offered by Education Department staff. Graduate docents are offered an extensive programme of continuing education which includes lectures, field trips, research and study groups, and training for special exhibitions – all of which keep docents expert in their fields.

The Oakland Museum of California brings to mind the descriptions of the first ever museums of ancient times – centres of learning open to all, dedicated to self-directed education and intellectual pursuits. The museum is indeed a place in which to muse. The feel and the ethos of the organisation are like that of a community centre – a resource and a place in which to meet others. It resembles many a university campus with its safe, secure, low building and green walkways visible from most of the museum's galleries.

However, docents are required to muse in a somewhat more disciplined and formal way than most of the visitors. Induction training involves one semester of basic subject training, either art, history, or natural sciences, followed by two semesters in the gallery. From September to February, with two weeks off for Christmas, there are weekly classes with exams every six to seven weeks. A paper must be written at the end of each term, and field trips usually take place about once a month. The practical on-gallery training begins in March.

Along with the standard texts that are used, each docent develops his/her own tour techniques, learning from others and from research that is presented in class. Over the Summer each individual brings his/her own personal group for a tour. This tour is supervised by a curator who has taught the docent and who then gives feedback on the final tours. Each of the three galleries has a comprehensive docent manual, providing docents with practical details on exhibit production and offering more unusual interpretative techniques.

Of all the volunteers, docents are more plentiful and have a higher profile than other volunteers; however, volunteers work in almost every part of the museum – even in the restaurant. In fact, the kitchen was for a while run entirely by volunteers. Unfortunately, offering only one waitress-served meal a day for five days a week, it did not make a profit. Now it is run by paid staff who have successfully changed the catering services and are now making a profit from their activities. However, volunteers' contributions are still valued and needed, and a small team regularly comes in and helps out in specific areas. According to the catering manager, it was difficult when the paid catering company was first brought in but they now work together with the volunteers. Some volunteers come in early and slice and dice; others help out at the front counter. Other volunteers make cookies, and when they are sold it is always advertised that they are the product of volunteers' work.

A regular commitment of the volunteer catering staff is serving tea to the senior citizens who come in for special Thursday morning docent tours. Most of the volunteers are women in their 50s to 70s. Their work is administered by the Food Service Council. Volunteers who wait on the tables in the evenings and for special events earn 20 per cent of the catering fees. These fees go directly back into the budget run by the Food Service Council and are spent on equipment for the kitchen and restaurant. This has allowed the purchase of articles such as the stained glass window in the café and the umbrellas outside that shade visitors from the sun.

The Collectors' Gallery is staffed entirely by volunteers. It offers works by contemporary Californian Bay artists and craftspeople. Pieces may be rented or purchased, and artists take 30 per cent commission. The art forms displayed cover all types of art, arts and crafts, prints and photographs, painting and drawing and jewellery making, and each month the gallery focuses on a different artist. One of the museum's objectives is to offer local artists a place in which to show and sell their work. The gallery is there to educate the public about art, and give artists a chance to exhibit their art alongside the city's permanent art collection. The volunteers work in a place where they meet interesting people and are able to gain administration to all art shows and attend the museum lectures for free. Once again, all the procedures for sales and for managing the shop are well documented to make it easy for new volunteers to understand the purpose and aims of the gallery and to maintain the standards of service that the gallery demands.

Education Department volunteers provide a supportive, active team to implement programmes that have been planned by the Education Department in consultation with various community groups. The numbers of volunteers and their particular duties varies and depends on the particular events. For example, one particular event, 'The Day of the Dead' programme, celebrating an annual Mexican festival, was developed almost entirely by 12 Latino volunteers for whom the festival played an integral part in their culture. Volunteers from the community then worked as Community Guides for the exhibition. Community Guides attend three training sessions and then provide guided tours of selected special exhibitions.

Education Department volunteers also assist with implementing family programmes, festivals and other public events. Youths, as well as adults, work as volunteers for the department. The fourth and final council, the Museum Services Council, as its name indicates, recruits and administers the work of the volunteers who give out information at the desks, help administer events, etc.

The rigorous training demands and the high standards set for the docents do have certain drawbacks. First, the volunteers tend to have a narrow demographic profile – being mostly retired people who have the time to offer. Until recently, the majority of volunteers in the Collectors' Gallery have been women; but it is becoming increasingly hard to staff the gallery as a growing proportion of the local population who used to volunteer are now going back to paid work, women in particular. However, although recognised as drawbacks, these matters have not yet posed any real problems.

For the 1,300 volunteers there is a paid Docent Co-ordinator, a Special Event/tour Co-ordinator, and a Volunteer Co-ordinator.

4.2 Science North, Sudbury, Ontario, Canada: responding to a need in the community

> The mission of Science North is to provide stimulating learning opportunities throughout Northern Ontario, in English and in French, for both residents and tourists, which involve people in the relationships between science and technology and everyday life with a northern emphasis.
>
> (Science North, 1994a)

Canadian clear blue skies, expanses of glistening water, and comfortable air-conditioned buildings are first and lasting impressions of Science North. Its location is simply stunning, and the varied combination of amenities and visitor attractions highlight the natural attractions of Northern Ontario. The heavy industry that once fuelled the city of Sudbury has been taken over by a thriving service industry; Science North is a major tourist attraction of the province.

For the visitor arriving in Sudbury by bus from Toronto four hours south, Science North could not go unnoticed or unknown. Two giant stainless steel snowflake-shaped buildings make Science North a modern landmark of the city; large billboards strategically positioned on the roadside unashamedly advertise its assets.

For the early part of this century, Sudbury relied on nickel-mining for most of its livelihood. Sudbury certainly demonstrates a creative approach to identifying new products and finding new markets for them: when the price of nickel began to drop, Sudbury discovered many new uses of nickel and marketed it with renewed purpose. Nickel was marketed as a useful mineral in its own right. When the production of both copper and nickel slowed down, the town, in response to the growing economy of the service industries, began to focus on and market a different natural resource. What had previously been considered as a dirty mining town was cleverly re-landscaped into an attractive city park and science centre. A leading tourist attraction was created, which simultaneously provided an educational resource for the whole of Northern Ontario.

What we now see as an established picturesque park has an interesting history which has shaped the economy and welfare of Northern Ontario for many years. The site bears little resemblance to the barren lifeless landscape that was an inevitable consequence of early twentieth-century mining techniques. New technologies make mining safer and more environmentally friendly, allowing it to continue almost unseen well below ground, controlling the environmental damage and reducing the personal risks to its workers.

So what are these varied amenities and assets of which Science North so loudly boasts? A science centre offering science shows, workshops and novel hands-on interactive exhibits, an Imax® cinema, a 3-D cinema, the big nickel mine, and a beautiful lake with boats to hire. A large family restaurant that is open most evenings overlooks the lake. Special seasonal events highlight the centre's unique environment. Nature trails are provided around the lakeside, and other outdoor activities are held on one of the roof terraces leading directly off the public galleries.

In 1993/4 Science North's operating budget was $5.5 million – 34 per cent self-generated and 66 per cent from the government. The centre welcomes hundreds of thousands of visitors each year and reached an additional 65,000 with its extensive outreach programme in 1993/4. Like many other museums and science centres, Science North had to cut back on full-time staff and increase the number of contract workers. The human resource strategy reflects this continuum of change in the work-force and acknowledges a need to invest in human resource development. In order to facilitate this, a staff task force consulted all staff and developed a human resource value statement for the organisation.

'Every employee and volunteer at Science North has a responsibility to treat others fairly and to communicate openly and honestly in an environment of mutual respect, trust and continual learning' (Science North, 1994b). The human resource goals suggested by this value statement involve an emphasis on communication, professional development, and performance management and reward. The volunteer programme at Science North is a reflection of the strong commitment to outreach into the community and to investing in human resources.

Although volunteers had played an active role in the museum since its opening in 1984, it was three years later that staff identified and recognised that the volunteers and the museum would benefit from a more co-ordinated approach to the management of volunteers. The Manager of Volunteers developed and encouraged a more rigorous approach to volunteer management.

The centre's personal style is impressive. From the full-time receptionists of the admission tills to the animal keepers, all the staff give the impression that they are truly enjoying their jobs. A huge team of gallery Explainers is on site to assist visitors to participate and understand. Clever light-hearted science shows are performed in an intimate, steeply raked circular theatre. Interactions with staff and conversations centre on standard visitor requests such as directions to specific facilities and explanations of nearby exhibits. The professional paid Explainer staff seem to take pride in their job and demonstrate a belief in the organisation. Their scientific knowledge and overall familiarity with the centre's facilities, history and management is indicative of a well-managed and motivated work-force. All the floor staff appeared aware of one another's skills and whereabouts at all times.

The human resource value statement formally acknowledges and recognises the centre's commitment to training and individual development: 'The centre will pursue opportunities to offer staff a flexible work environment which matches individual wishes with operation needs. These may include flexible hours, compressed work weeks, or a benefits menu' (Science North, 1994b). Written reports and visitor guides uphold the centre's philosophy towards its staff: 'The talents and time of its people are Science North's most valuable assets' (Science North, 1993: 18).

The Manager of Volunteer's own publication on volunteer management introduces the concepts and principles behind the practices:

> Long before it opened its doors to the public in 1984, Science North made a commitment to develop a vigorous volunteer program. It was not a matter of seeking cheap labour; as any successful volunteer program never is. Rather it was an opportunity for Science North to make a contribution to the people of the Sudbury region, a contribution of the space, expertise, equipment and ambience that make up this science centre.
>
> The program offers to the people of Sudbury and area a chance to share their knowledge, their interests and their enthusiasm with the staff and visitors to the science centre. Volunteers while working side by side with staff and performing an infinite variety of useful jobs are also an important customer group at Science North. They pay to come to Science North using valuable time as currency. It is Science North's obligation to provide them with an educational and entertaining experience which justifies their investment.
>
> Only through a well managed volunteer program can volunteers receive the maximum enjoyment from their time at Science North. They bring with them riches of experience, energy, and curiosity. The Science Centre contributes its knowledge, equipment and accessibility. Together these form a winning combination of unlimited potential for enhancing community life in Northern Ontario.
>
> (Lalande, 1989)

A few statistics fill in the picture of the Volunteer Programme as of April 1996:

- approximately 300 volunteers work in the centre;
- most volunteers spend between two and six hours per week at Science North;
- between May 1995 and April 1996, volunteers contributed over 21,000 hours;
- on average there are 10–12 volunteers a day;
- 45 per cent of volunteers are bilingual;
- teen volunteers contribute over 5,000 hours yearly.

The volunteer team can be split into two principal groups – the Youth Programme and the Adult Volunteer Team.

Volunteer positions have developed with the presenting skills of the volunteer applicants. For example, a retired couple had for the last few years been giving the museum horticultural advice on gardens and plants inside and around the buildings, and assisted in the maintenance of all the plants, particularly those in the building. As a great proportion of Science North's walls are glass, the gardens and plants are a feature of the centre. Colourful indoor plants flourish in the sunlight and the gardens are visible from most parts of the galleries. Volunteer gardeners actually create (by giving advice) and implement (through their gardening activities) in this position.

More often than not, volunteers are restricted in their activities by people's assumptions about what and who volunteers are. 'Volunteers are not just people with nothing better to do; they're professional, students, active retirees – we've got to meet their schedules' (Livingston as quoted by Happer, 1994: 9).

Science North's 'swap shop' is an excellent example of how to integrate and deploy the specialist skills of volunteers in an appropriate area. Visitors are encouraged to bring in rocks, shells, and fossils that they have collected and trade them for objects contained in Science North's collection. Most people probably get excited at the concept of finding a rare sample of a mineral and bringing it to the attention of a worthy scholar. Seeing cases full of glistening minerals with staff and volunteers on hand to talk about the minerals and answer special questions seems to incite many visitors to go outside and go collecting. Objects brought in are identified by staff and/or volunteers and, depending on their rarity or in some cases the effort that the visitor made in collecting them, so many points are assigned to the object. Points can be used to buy/exchange for other natural objects in the swap shop. Valuing particular objects with a story and context personal to the collector encourages visitors to gain understanding of the limited mineral resources and the importance of conservation of the natural environment. Volunteers who work in the swap shop area tend to be retired people with an interest in geology who want to use and develop their skills and knowledge while benefiting others. Science North has set up swap shops in Northern Ontario communities. These shops are in public libraries, community centres and museums. They are operated by volunteers from the various towns.

Adult volunteers are asked to wear blue overcoats of the same style as, but a shade lighter than, those of the paid staff. Some adult volunteers work at home, in their workshops, building, repairing and renovating small exhibits. Retired machinists, carpenters and electricians enjoy the creative work that is involved. The staff ensures that volunteers are included from the inception of all new projects.

Science North has a multi-level Youth Programme. The Summer Customer Service Team assist staff with their regular, core daily activities such as ensuring that the audience is seated in time for the science shows or assisting demonstrators, and also provide additional activity stations such as offering younger visitors a colourful rubber hand stamp, entertaining visitors in line-ups, pet-sitting for travellers with pets, assisting in the parking lot and operating the lost children area. The thinking behind these teen positions is that both the centre and the teens gain. The job description states that: 'Teens participate in a variety of interactive science activities for visitors, working a two-week session with a group. Skills strengthened are public speaking, performing, work skills, and presentation.'

Weekend work is available during the Autumn and Winter. Teens will be recommended to advance to the science area after successful completion of an eight-month, half-day Saturday programme. The programme develops job skills, public skills and customer service skills. Successful completion demands regular attendance and recommendations from staff. Older, experienced teens can get involved in the training of new teen volunteers, assist in organising social events and attend update sessions with volunteers. This progressive, graded system of teen volunteer opportunities has developed over the years. Weekend positions for teens were introduced relatively recently, in 1993. The teen teams wear bright turquoise Science North t-shirts which label them as junior uniformed staff.

One of the major attractions of volunteering at Science North is that it is less demanding than community welfare work; this seems to be a result of the well-defined time-commitments that are required. In addition to seeking out volunteers whose daily jobs require skills and knowledge related to the exhibits or programmes, an institution might also want to accommodate preferences for short-term time-commitments. Specific projects with known time-frames can be very appealing on both sides (Happer 1994).

Science North, although an international tourist attraction, is simultaneously a local amenity. The centre's outreach programme provides a valuable educational service to isolated villages as far north as Red Lake (approx. 1,000 km from Sudbury). Income from tourists helps to sustain and finance its educational service in the province directly through admission charges and indirectly through other expenditure. Volunteering offers the local community ways in which to develop their skills while simultaneously providing a resource that directly supports the centre's mission.

Most of the teenagers have a splendid time revelling in the social interactions that are an essential part of regular work and customer service, and enjoying the respect and kudos of being a uniformed member of staff in a high-profile organisation. Teens do, of course, demand and require close supervision and management, but rewards are reaped by both sides.

4.3 Denver Museum of Natural History, Denver, Colorado, USA: a massive programme with excellent training and communications

> Founded in 1900, the Denver Museum of Natural History serves its diverse community by promoting the study, understanding and

enjoyment of nature, the universe, and human cultures in an easily
accessible and visitor-sensitive manner.

(Denver Museum of Natural History, 1994: 3)

In December 1897, a group of leading Denverites gathered together for the
purpose of establishing a museum and library of natural history. Three years
later, in December 1900, the museum was incorporated as the Colorado
Museum of Natural History. By 1901, construction of the building began at the
east end of the then barren and treeless City Park; the stately, three-storey,
8,600-square-foot museum building was opened to the public in 1908. Over the
years, numerous additions have been made to the building. Today it covers
500,896 square feet. The Denver Museum of Natural History welcomes over
1.5 million visitors each year and is now the third-largest natural history
museum in the United States. Over 200 paid staff are supplemented by over
3,500 volunteers.

Before 1987, an effective volunteers programme had been run entirely by
volunteers, with no formal structure. There were no job descriptions for
volunteers and no member of staff responsible for their activities. Following a
temporary exhibition requiring 2,000 volunteers, it became apparent that
a more structured approach would be beneficial; the first full-time Manager of
Volunteer Services, Sarah Christian, was employed. Within 10 years, she had
set up an effective infrastructure that is capable of deploying 3,500 volunteers.
Every month there are now 1,500–1,800 active volunteers, and blockbuster
temporary exhibits can easily bring in an additional 1,500. In 1993, volunteers
gave the museum 170,344 hours of work. The Manager of Volunteer Services
works full-time alongside three other Volunteer Supervisors: one for all
Education Division volunteers, another to co-ordinate and manage all the
volunteers working in travelling exhibitions, and another to oversee the
volunteers working in all the visitor services – front-of-house, at the information
desk, and at the schools entrance.

How did the Manager of Volunteer Services go about the daunting task of
setting up and enforcing an infrastructure on an established volunteer
programme? With no specific role to follow, she began by talking to the staff
to gain an understanding of how the museum operated, and also to get to
know the staff and their specific responsibilities, and ultimately to get a feel
for potential areas of volunteer activity. She interviewed the staff personally,
asking them: 'What do you do?', 'What do you like and dislike about your
job?', 'Could you delegate any part of your job?', 'If so, what would it be?'.
Careful consideration was given to what the staff said. It was the task of the
Manager of Volunteer Services to decide if a combination of the tasks and areas
of work that the staff were willing to delegate could be made the substance of
a proper volunteer position. The question she asked herself was what kind of
a job would it be – not just envelope stuffing. As she said: 'The difficulty was
that staff had to be willing to really delegate.' (Sarah Christian in interview.)

The Manager of Volunteer Services is now responsible for the recruitment and
training of the 3,500 volunteers in the museum. Many of the procedures are,

in fact, run and managed by the different departments and by the volunteers themselves. A team of eight volunteers has been trained to do all of the initial screening. All the final interviewing and special training is organised and managed by the appropriate Volunteer Supervisor for the job.

Denver Museum of Natural History is such a high-profile institution that, by and large, recruitment is done by word of mouth and through membership. Two to three applications are received each day from the Denver community and the museum's pool of 35,000 members. Occasionally there are targeted recruitment exercises looking for people with particular skills. These have been used to recruit security staff targeting specifically retired security persons through ex-policemen or specific social clubs. Volunteer applicants are expected to complete an application form and they are then invited to meet with one of the placement counsellors for an interview. The object of the interview is twofold – the museum wants to find the best fit of volunteer to the job whilst giving the volunteers the kind of jobs that they want. The museum learns something of the volunteer's motivation in volunteering, whilst the volunteer finds out about the organisation and the opportunities available.

On meeting one of the placement counsellors, volunteers are asked to select two or three areas that they are interested in. A report from the placement counsellor is then sent to the appropriate volunteer supervisors. If all goes well, a second interview is arranged with one of the Volunteer Supervisors. A decision is made between the volunteer and the supervisor regarding where the volunteer will work.

Volunteers are expected to sign in every day at the Volunteer Office. The Volunteer Office is, in fact, a series of interlinking offices and lounges adjacent to the schools entrance. There is a lounge, kitchen facilities, and lockers; a bulletin board serves as a central communication point.

Orientation for all staff was initiated by the Volunteer Office. The Manager of Volunteer Services and the Manager of Visitor Services run orientation classes together. The classes include a slide show of the history of the museum, explanations of the organisational chart and a walking tour of the building and its facilities. There is a limit of 36 persons per session. These training sessions are held every month excluding December. Accompanying the training is a volunteer and staff handbook, shared by both paid and voluntary staff. Certain sections are split as appropriate for staff and volunteers – such as those dealing with benefits and opportunities. Other sections are applicable to the staff and volunteers equally – such as those describing the museum's staff structure, the media policy and security procedures. Of particular interest is the section on professionalism, which is applicable to both staff and volunteers: it states clearly what values and standards the staff and volunteers agree to, and in turn what they should expect from the museum. For example, staff and volunteers are expected to agree to:

- Consider their work a serious professional commitment and view the position as valid and important;

- Follow the position description and accept supervision;
- Represent the museum at all times in an appropriate and responsible manner.

Volunteer and staff may expect to:

- Work at a position that is worthwhile and challenging with freedom to use existing skills and/or develop new ones;
- Receive periodic feedback;
- Be involved or represented in decisions that affect you.

(Denver Museum of Natural History, 1944)

To all intents and purposes, this is a mutual service agreement between the museum and the volunteer. Apart from this, there is no actual paper contract that is signed except in areas where a high degree of labour-intensive training is required, such as for the Education Division docents. These volunteers are asked to sign a contract for one school year.

This clear statement of the museum's expectations of professionalism and what, in turn, the volunteer and staff should expect and receive from the museum is comparable to Science North's human resource value statement discussed in the previous case study. Both organisations have decided that it is important to state the organisations' standards and mission with regard to the management of one of their most valuable resources – the people that work there.

One of the services that the Volunteer Office provides to staff is training on how to manage volunteers: this includes sessions on motivation, recognition within the department, evaluation and constructive criticism. These sessions have all been well received by staff.

Christian sees the volunteer office as a 'people broker'. Once the volunteer is placed, he or she becomes part of that specific department. The Volunteer Office continues to play a central role in motivating and recognising the work of volunteers; in a way comparable to that of a senior human resource manager, she is responsible for devising appropriate staff selection, benefits, training and conditions. Christian views the volunteer office as a facilitator and resource for volunteers and Volunteer Supervisors. Staff and volunteers are encouraged to resolve issues between themselves, and Christian prefers to offer advice, as and when requested. In her words: 'The institution is very dedicated to using volunteers. Staff really have the picture that their work can only be enhanced by working with volunteers' (Sarah Christian in interview).

Was there any bad feeling between the staff and volunteers as the volunteer programme had been developed into a huge programme outnumbering paid staff? There did not seem to have been any resistance to volunteers, only the inevitable misunderstandings as staff learnt about how to manage volunteers and delegate appropriate tasks. 'The automatic response from staff was positive. It meant expansion – the museum could do more. Staff do not find it in any way threatening working with volunteers' (ibid.).

It is a tribute to the contribution of volunteers and an indication of the excellence of the strategic management of this valuable resource that the key defining document of the organisation includes the activities of the volunteers' programme. The 'Operating Plan of the Denver Museum', which clearly lists the museum's goals and objectives, makes specific mention of the management and the development of volunteers. Among the museum's stated goals (which are categorised under the headings: 'Museum education, audience, management, financial resources') is the following management goal: 'Operate a well managed museum through the effective and diverse team of trustees, staff and volunteers.' Among the specific objectives listed within this section are:

- promote an institutional culture supportive of diversity, co-operation, communication and productivity and creativity;
- enhance communication among and between volunteers and staff in all departments and the museum as a whole;
- support the professional development of staff and volunteers;
- refine new employee and volunteer orientation program;
- develop a recognition program that rewards outstanding visitor service, credibility enhancement, cost savings and other significant staff and volunteer contributions.

Denver is not the biggest museum in America when measured by visitor numbers, turnover, or floor area; but it has by far the highest ratio of volunteers to staff. It treats the volunteers both as an audience and as a resource.

Bigger is not necessarily better, and Christian is acutely aware of how much staff time is required to recruit, train, and manage the volunteers. However, the fact is that with a clear business acumen (that demands that the capital investment and high running costs of such a large programme be constantly set against the ultimate long-term pay-off), the museum has created a highly successful and profitable volunteer programme.

To give an example of how quickly Christian has developed the volunteer activities with her purposeful and sensitive management, the Palaeontology Department has come from having no volunteers in 1987 to currently having 300 volunteers who do work equivalent to that of 15 full-time members of staff.

All departments except Finance now take on volunteers. In the beginning, some departments simply did not want to work with volunteers; there were others where Christian would not place volunteers until she felt confident that the staff appreciated that volunteers were accountable to the same performance standards as paid staff, and had similar expectations of the museum to those of any member of staff.

Volunteers are aged between 14 and 94. Opportunities for the teenagers are focused in the Summer and at weekends. Teenagers work in most of the different departments of the museum including the curatorial divisions; they act as interpreters with the vast education collections which include anything from whale bones to mounted taxidermy. They push touch-carts around the galleries which allow visitors to touch real things from the Education Collection and ask about them. These carts are always staffed by volunteers rather than paid staff.

Although the museum is located in a fairly ethnically diverse area, volunteers currently do not come from all the ethnic minorities in the proportions of the local community. This is an issue that is constantly being worked upon. People volunteer when their needs are met: the volunteer database indicates that current volunteers are predominantly well-educated, middle- to upper-class Caucasians who have the leisure time to give. The museum tries to make the volunteer programme as flexible as possible in order to attract a diverse volunteer team representative of the local community. Some positions demand a regular commitment and some do not: front-of-house and information desk volunteers can do the job effectively working only one or two weekends a month. This allows people who are in full-time employment to volunteer and give just one or two Saturdays per month.

There is a high retention of volunteers: 60 per cent of volunteers have been at the Denver Museum for three years or more. Sarah Christian believes that the reason people stay this long is that they are treated appropriately. There is always some new and different opportunity on the horizon, and there are many incentives and a fairly extensive benefits package.

Recognition lunches and dinners are arranged: around $17,000 is spent on this every year. There is an awards banquet that recognises volunteers for their contributions. Staff and trustees are invited and the final number of people at the dinners is between 500 and 600 at each sitting, 25 per cent of whom are staff. All these activities are very much supported by the trustees. There are other non-agenda social events throughout the year. Ongoing education is provided for volunteers and opportunities are constantly offered for them to learn new skills. Curator lunches and quarterly behind-the-scenes tours are organised by the Manager of Volunteer Services for small groups, enabling them to spend one or two hours with individual curators.

With volunteers, the learning process is slower than for full-time staff due to the volunteers shorter working hours, typically from four to eight hours a week. Some volunteers do come with highly applicable specialised skills and may also be able to give slightly longer and regular time commitments. It does, of course, take up staff time to train and recognise the volunteers; but when they come to understand that training volunteers is an opportunity to show their speciality and increase understanding, the paid staff want to do more. Such training harnesses team spirit and it is a way to create a general understanding among all staff of the institution.

The training for docents is longer and more in-depth than that of other volunteers. Initial docent training covers presentation styles, crowd management, discipline, children's learning, and general teacher training. Docents are required to attend 25 to 30 hours of training, and are then assigned a referral docent with whom to tour and model for the first couple of months. Retraining is obligatory for docents each year. Seasoned volunteers and staff evaluate the docents and there is ongoing evaluation plus self-evaluation in order to maintain the high standards.

The focus of this case study has been on the infrastructure and practices that have been used to manage a volunteer programme of over 3,500 people who, in a year, provide the full-time equivalent of over 130 staff. It indicates what is possible with good management practices.

4.4 The Museum of Science, Boston, Massachusetts, USA: breadth of opportunities for volunteers and good supervision

The Mission of the Museum of Science is to stimulate interest in and further understanding of science and technology and their importance for individuals and society. To accompany this educational Mission, the staff, volunteers, Overseers and Trustees of the museum are dedicated to attracting the broadest possible spectrum of participants and involving them in activities, exhibits and programs which will:

- encourage curiosity questioning and exploration;
- inform and educate;
- enhance a sense of personal achievement in learning;
- respect individual interests, backgrounds and abilities; and
- promote life-long learning and informed and active citizenship.

All this is offered in the spirit that learning is exciting and fun at the Museum of Science.

(Museum of Science, 1993: 3)

The Museum of Science in Boston is a private not-for-profit, informal, educational institution founded in 1830. From its opening in a temporary building on its present site in February 1950, the museum's history has been one of providing excellent scientific exhibits and programmes for the public. Although the Museum of Science now houses predominantly interactive exhibits, as opposed to exhibitions around objects, the museum grew from the Boston Society of Natural History and has, therefore, a large collection of objects (over 30,000 predominantly in natural history, but also in art and cultural history). These objects are designated primarily as teaching collections, not for research. They are used for educational activities encompassing exhibits, lectures, classes, demonstrations, reference services, and other programmes.

The facilities of the Museum of Science and the public programmes are vast and varied. Three full days in the museum were sufficient only to glimpse most of the galleries. The museum has an operating budget of approximately $22 million: some 90 per cent of this is generated from earned income. There were 230 full-time-equivalent employees in the 1995/6 financial year, complemented by over 65,000 volunteers hours – the equivalent of 36 full-time staff.

From the mission statement itself it is not surprising that a volunteer programme plays an integral part in the museum's day-to-day business. The last aim sums up the basic achievements of well-run museum volunteer programmes. They promote life-long learning for the volunteer and simultaneously for the visitor, and encourage active citizenship. Volunteers work in almost all museum departments – front-of-house and behind the scenes.

Volunteers have been at the Boston Museum of Science for 37 years, starting out with a group of primarily middle-aged, middle-class women. Now the Volunteer Office is the central administrative office for over 600 volunteers. The Volunteer Co-ordinator's job is to work out appropriate job descriptions, recruit volunteers, maintain the service, find jobs for volunteers, ensure that staff have enough volunteers, recognise the volunteers, and attend to all the necessary administration. The Volunteer Office remains the central office for changes in jobs and so on. To keep track of volunteers' hours, it is required that they sign in and out. A database of the volunteers' hours is kept; they get their awards according to how many hours they give.

Recruitment is carried out in many different ways – through newspapers in the city and local districts via press releases; through a mailing list of colleges who have courses in science and education; through guidance counsellors and science teachers in high schools. The best mode of recruitment has been by word of mouth – through friends and relatives.

Volunteer opportunities are available as interpreters in the galleries of the Discovery Centre, the Human Body Discovery Space, and the Computer Discovery Centre. Volunteers also help out in all the offices, including the Volunteer Office itself; the Volunteer Office actually organises fund-raising events.

A volunteer information pack is sent out to each new volunteer explaining opportunities that are available. There is a general initial meeting in the Volunteer Office from which volunteers are assigned to whatever area they are to work in. This central office also acts as the personnel office for volunteers screening. Once someone has been accepted to volunteer, they attend an initial orientation training workshop given by the Volunteer Office. They then receive on-the-job training from a specific department for two to six weeks depending on the area of work involved.

Supervisors must evaluate volunteers after the initial six weeks and once every six months. Although many volunteers are experts in the areas they are working on, they still want feedback from the permanent paid staff. They are there to get something out of the experience: they want support. Some volunteers wonder why the museum evaluates them; but most like it. There are definitely high standards to meet, and volunteers must be told if they are not meeting these standards. After all, the public does not know whether the staff they see working are voluntary or salaried, although volunteers wear blue lab coats or aprons, whereas paid staff usually wear t-shirts, sweatshirts, or laboratory coats. The Volunteer Office is willing to fire people if they are problematic. It is made clear that it is rude and unacceptable simply not to show up for an agreed shift.

The museum could not survive without volunteers. They do a great deal of work, and that is now accepted; but the recognition and acceptance took a long time to evolve. The relationship between paid staff and volunteers is not now much of a problem, but it used to be. The most difficult problem has been that of staff thinking that volunteers would be unreliable. It has been found, however, that if high expectations are set by staff for volunteers (through clear job descriptions, training, and supervision), volunteers do their jobs well and meet the expectations set by staff. Most volunteers do not want to get paid; they are not there to develop careers as museum professionals. Rather, they want to be there for different reasons – socialising, wanting to 'give something back', and all sorts of other reasons. Staff are now trained to work with volunteers.

Volunteers in Boston are loyal and keep coming regularly. Many volunteers help out on a routine basis; others are on reserve lists to be called for special events. A key feature in generating such loyalty is the respect, feedback, and recognition by paid staff to volunteers. Paid staff must appreciate that volunteers work in their own time out of choice.

To give due recognition to the volunteers, there is an annual dinner party with awards for hours of service. Many benefits are also available for volunteers such as special preview nights at the Omni Theatre. For national volunteer week, there is a special banner in the lobby to welcome them. The Volunteer Office tries to remember all the volunteers, i.e., by sending them Valentine cards that their supervisors have signed.

At the beginning of the 37 years of the volunteer programme, there were docents leading people around the museum. Then there was a programme in which every day a group of specialist volunteers gave expert talks on topics. There was, however, a problem in that the volunteers only talked about one topic. So next came the creation of Discovery Spaces with more flexible staff moving around interactive exhibits rather than remaining in one place as an expert. Visitors liked these areas. There have now been 15 years of interactive discovery areas staffed by volunteers.

In the interpretation programme for life sciences and physical sciences it was found to be better to separate the volunteers into groups; to teach a volunteer to be fluent in all subjects was impossible. Volunteers are trained separately; once a month, they all meet together.

In the Human Body Discovery Space the museum tries to teach volunteers the big ideas and concepts of the subject areas and their consequences, rather than specific facts. Such concepts include:

- evolution, adaptation, natural selection;
- ecology;
- the flow of matter and energy through the universe;
- cell biology and the biochemistry of cells.

With appropriate training, the volunteers can work in the galleries with a few objects and, through talking to visitors, relate those objects to the bigger ideas embodied in the above themes. They are also capable of taking the basic tools and methodology of the subjects and applying them to the exhibits, offering the visitor assistance with whatever he or she needs. In short, there has been a change in attitude and expectation of the volunteer from someone who is an expert in a scientific subject to someone who is simply capable of understanding the big concepts underlying science, and has the ability and confidence to talk about them. This approach challenges the pressure to script and schedule everything, and emphasises individual learning and teaching. The conversations that take place during tea and coffee breaks have been changing.

It has been found necessary to define clearly what staff do and what volunteers do. Volunteers cannot all be expected to do exactly the same thing: some volunteers are extraordinarily skilled in specific areas. The Boston volunteer programme decided to aim really high. The museum started by accepting non-scientific retirees for the interactive discovery areas now it does not accept adult volunteers without some kind of basic scientific background. The paid staff now look at volunteers as a pool of talent and expertise. It used to be that volunteers were all non-working women; now the museum has a better mix of people. The museum expects, and now demands, people who really love talking about science.

Volunteers do the in-gallery informal interpretation and hosting; the paid staff do all the educational programmes. In the Discovery Centre, for example, there are 100 volunteers assigned to work in the area. Some volunteers have been working there for 10 years. Now the Discovery Centre can deploy around six volunteers per session – ideally with people at specific areas and a floater or two.

Volunteers are aged from 14 upwards. The teenagers are encouraged to work with children and act as role models for them. Some volunteers are supported by their companies; others are school teachers and hospital staff. One volunteer is a doctor who developed an exhibit for the gallery.

In addition to the initial training, there is a daily briefing session for volunteers with workshop activity, video, discussion, varied teaching methods – on subjects such as plate tectonics, rocks and minerals, skeleton and bone physiology, language and terminology, on suggested activities, on structuring explanations/comparisons, and on relating one thing to another. The museum staff tried to think of a way to train volunteers in order to ensure that they were given basic information; now they have a comprehensive checklist covering:

- fire safety;
- internal procedures and practices;
- basic knowledge needed to function.

Theoretical training is mixed with floor work. Each volunteer is paired with a companion and with an intern. In the first week, they do not wear uniforms but just watch, observing and working on some areas that do not need much knowledge such as at the gate or desk area. Another part of the organiser's responsibility is being sure that the new volunteers are out on the floor seeing different museum events. The volunteers choose what events they want to go to each day, and are given a form to fill out designed to get the volunteer to watch critically, try to learn from others' appropriate interpretation methods, and encourage sensitivity to the demonstrator and the audience. Each volunteer has a folder of their training progress. A number of topic packs have been put together by paid staff especially for volunteers; these give information and point up the links between galleries and interactive discovery areas. The volunteers are given a handbook for the Discovery Centre and topic packs to add to their own handbooks. There is a rolling programme of training and briefings. New volunteers can learn from topic packs, briefings which vary for specific inter- active techniques, general updates about the museum, and looking around the museum themselves.

The Discovery Centre can be booked on Tuesdays, Wednesdays, and Thursdays. All school parties are greeted and an area is reserved for briefings that are given before and after the visit to the Discovery Centre for no longer than 10 minutes. Volunteers enjoy working with school groups because they have a clear focus.

Volunteers are classed and referred to as 'staff'. The museum management thinks of them as unpaid employees having a job description and having to fit basic requirements for a job. The museum has in the past turned volunteers away. In the recruitment process they come in to be screened and to meet the supervisors, most of whom ask the volunteers what they themselves hope to gain from a position. If it is known what people come for, it is possible to understand them and place them in the appropriate positions. It is really important to know why the volunteers are there.

The museum is working to diversify the volunteer group. Volunteers currently come from all over eastern Massachusetts – some people from 30–50 miles away. The demographic profile of the volunteers used to be dominated by white, retired, middle-class people. The museum has made a real effort to diversify this profile in terms of educational background and origin, occupation/ profession, ethnicity, and so on.

The museum works extensively with college students and high school students; volunteers take the young visitors onto the galleries and learn to respect and appreciate the visitors and one another. They talk to the children as peers. Some older volunteers do not want to work with high school students; they see them as being too great a responsibility and as detracting from the attention given to the younger visitors.

The key perception in the Boston Museum of Science is that volunteers need to feel needed; they need to feel special and be recognised behind the scenes. So successful has the museum been in maintaining this philosophy that over the last 37 years close to 20,000 volunteers have given approximately 2.5 million hours of service to the museum.

4.5 The University of Toronto School of Continuing Studies: preparation of potential interpreters as a form of adult education

An emerging theme in the preceding case studies, and of this book as a whole, is that the training needed for people to act as effective museum interpreters is itself a valuable form of education for volunteers. This final case study focuses on a course set up as an introductory course for would-be docents. When asked by the University of Toronto School of Continuing Studies (UFT SCS), museums in southern Ontario recognised that more volunteer educators would be needed. Many museums were experiencing a shortage of appropriately skilled and diverse applicants. A Steering Committee formed by the UFT SCS carefully planned a course of action to try to alleviate this problem by developing a training course for the volunteer museum educators.

The goals of the course were to attract a multicultural pool of potential docents/interpreters to the range of cultural institutions which support collections/exhibitions and train them in the roles and skills of docents/ interpreters within those institutions. The course was aimed at people with little or no guiding experience who liked to speak about culture and education, and to inform and interact with the public, and who might want to learn more about becoming a docent. As a guide, interpreter, or facilitator, the docent leads tours at museums, art galleries, artist-run centres and (natural science) interpretative centres. The course explores the roles and responsibilities of the docent. Its object is to increase participants' own capacity to enjoy visiting museums, galleries and historic sites while learning the basics of conducting tours, presentations, and activities for others. Work with an experienced instructor is designed to improve participants' understanding of cultural institutions, speaking in public, awareness of learning from objects, and anticipating the needs of the visitor. Observation, practice, and discussion were essential elements of the course. It included several class field trips to observe guided tours or activities in local cultural institutions. A course fee was charged which included admission charges to institutions visited (UFT SCS 1994 Calendar: 13).

The conception of this course had its roots in the Art Gallery of Ontario (AGO). In November 1989, the gallery's strategic plan for education indicated that there was going to be a need for more docents, and not only more docents but many more from among the communities which make up Toronto but who were not represented among the gallery's docents at that time. The Education Committee had recently been expanded and a representative from the UFT SCS had been added to the committee (see Demb and Castle, 1994).

The problem was not so much an absence of applicants but rather of a lack of candidates from non-traditional sources, and a lack of knowledge of the role of docent, especially in an art gallery, and/or the skills needed to meet the minimum requirements to enter the museum's own in-house docent training programme. The UFT SCS representative suggested offering an open admission programme financed by the tuition fees of the mature students interested in taking the course (ibid., 1994).

As the UFT SCS primarily offers non-credit, non-degree courses to the general public, the AGO decided that other institutions should be involved. Galleries, museums, and institutions like the Ontario Science Centre and the Metro Zoo were invited by SCS in February 1991 to assess the course to see if it could be developed for their individual needs. The response was excellent: 16 different institutions were represented by 28 docents or staff in a very open participative meeting. The goals were:

- to attract a new more broadly representative pool of docents and interpreters for cultural institutions in South-Central Ontario;
- to provide them with an understanding of the role of docents and the broad range of institutions throughout South-Central Ontario needing such volunteer interpreters;
- to provide them with the initial or entry skills required by these institutions;
- to provide an opportunity for potential docents to observe experienced docents on site.

In 1991/2, the course was launched. It was offered in alternate schedules at two UFT campuses and at an off-campus site in Eastern Ontario. The weekly daytime and evening courses both ran at the city centre (main) campus. Bi-weekly Saturday courses were offered from a suburban campus several miles from Toronto's centre. While the city centre courses ran successfully and each drew 17 registrants, the Saturday courses did not prove popular and failed to attract sufficient registrations to run. The introductory course was subsequently offered on the main campus each year through the Autumn of 1996. The evening schedule attracted more registrations than the daytime one, but the course failed to run only in one year, 1995. Enrolment in an intermediate course in 1994 was sufficient to run it that year but not sufficient to ensure it was offered in subsequent years. Enrolment in 1996 in the introductory course was low and so the course will not be offered until demand increases.

The course addressed the major concerns of, and overcame many of the minor problematic issues for, both docents and museums. A third party could provide introductory training on a non-judgmental basis, screening and guiding volunteers to the appropriate institutions. The participants self-selected themselves out of the docent volunteer stream if they did not want to continue; they could also choose at the beginning whether or not they would like to be evaluated and assessed to academic standards. Some participants were motivated to attend the course to enhance their own enjoyment of museums and cultural sites; others were planning for new jobs or volunteer opportunities that they might want to take up on retirement.

The course was not taken for academic credit, although students could be given Letters of Attendance if they attended at least 75 per cent of the sessions. Upon request and with the volunteer's consent, the instructor provided a reference to the museum. In this reference, the museum sought only an indication that the participant was dependable and really willing to learn.

As with many of the courses run at the UFT SCS, the curriculum was influenced by comments from students on course evaluation forms administered at the end of every course. The docent course, however, was unique in that it provided the structure and the goals and guided the direction, but did not control it. In the beginning, many experts were invited to lecture; then gradually less and less of this teaching technique was used, and the focus was finally to promote continuous learning by the students amongst themselves under the guidance of the instructor. This worked so well that one class (Autumn 1996) continued to meet informally after the course had finished, making presentations and sharing responses. The development of the course supports the androgogical theory of learning – namely, that students should learn how to learn from peers, professionals, and other human and material resources as well as working with the teachers; students should thus be more involved with the entire teaching and learning process, with the teacher's key role being that of facilitator rather than dispenser of knowledge (cf. Hiemestra, 1981).

Another example at UFT SCS is the physics/biology seminar which developed from student interest in the course entitled 'Understanding *A Brief History of Time*'. The physics professor gives several lectures to organise and initiate thinking along certain lines depending on the text selected for that year; the rest of the classes are run more like seminars, the teacher coming to the class more as a resource than an instructor. This course is offered in the science programme of the liberal studies area and attracts a fairly broad range of mature adults, most of whom have professional backgrounds in science, technology, medicine, or communication. It is not a formal part of the docent training programme.

This type of collaboration between museums and a university is just the type of good practice that we believe has a future. The UFT SCS continues to respond to enquiries from distant museums about how to set up similar programmes, and the school is currently exploring other forms of delivery.

The course syllabus was prepared for UFT SCS by Christine Castle in 1990 and approved by Constance Demb and the Steering Committee. It is revised annually. The objectives of the course state that participants will become able to:

1 identify the range and functions of the cultural institution, the roles of staff (paid/unpaid), and of professional organisations as well as sources of further research and professional development;
2 discuss the guiding principles, role and functions of the docent/ interpreter, past, present and future, and relate these to their personal goals and objectives as a docent/interpreter;
3 develop competence in public speaking and presentation skills and relate them to the interpretation of collections/exhibitions.
4 identify components of a tour or activity;
5 identify the primary audiences of the cultural institution, their characteristics and learning needs;
6 practise approaches to object-based learning and compare and contrast this method with other methods of learning within the cultural setting;

54

7 design and present a brief presentation applying the basic principles and/or skills of research, speaking, and object learning;
8 develop skills of constructive evaluation and apply these to tours of self and others;
9 build self-esteem and confidence;
10 have fun!

These objectives are realised through reading assignments, site visits, and sessions on *inter alia*: 'What Makes Cultural Institutions Special?', 'What is Guiding?', 'Public Speaking on Tour', 'Working with Objects', 'Working with People', 'Evaluation'. As recommended texts, participants are directed towards (1) Grinder and McCoy (1985) *The Good Guide: A Sourcebook for Interpreters, Docents and Tour Guides*, and (2) Regnier, Gross, and Zimmerman (1992) *The Interpreters' Guidebook: Techniques for Programs and Presentations*.

Before contacting an organisation that deploys docents, course participants are invited to consider the following questions from Kathleen Fletcher-Brown's (1987) *The 9 Keys to Successful Volunteer Programs*:

1 Why are you interested in volunteering at this site?
2 What personal experience have you had with the institution's area of specialisation (history, art, science, ecology, etc.)?
3 What would you like to get from this volunteer job?
4 What do you feel you can contribute to the institution's work?
5 What are your hobbies and interests?
6 Can you make a commitment of 6 months or a year to the volunteer job and related training requirements?
7 What would you like to know about the institution, its audiences, and the volunteer job itself?
8 How does the volunteer job fit in with your present life situation?

(Fletcher-Brown, 1987: 17)

Participants are then invited to approach any one of a list of 26 southern Ontario museums and centres, including: the Art Gallery of Hamilton; the Bradley Museum, Mississauga; the Metro Toronto Zoo; the Art Gallery of Ontario, Toronto; Burlington Cultural Centre; the McMichael Canadian Collection; the Ontario Science Centre; the Royal Botanical Gardens, Hamilton; the Ontario Agricultural Museum, Milton; the Pickering Museum; the Royal Ontario Museum, Toronto; the Todmorden Mills Museum, Toronto. Completion of the 'Guiding Tours' course is not, they are told, a guarantee of acceptance at any institution. However, the course instructor finds that, in their conversations with volunteer co-ordinators, educators, and curators at the various sites, it was seen as evidence of a very strong commitment to the field! Over the last six years, half of the 112 course graduates had become affiliated with a museum, gallery or park at the time of this study. The greatest number had gone to the AGO, with several going to other mid- to large-sized downtown institutions like the Bata Shoe Museum and the Royal Ontario Museum.

Institutional response to the impact of the docent training courses was mixed. At several sites, staff who had been highly involved in and supportive of the 1991 UFT SCS initiative had left and the institutional context for such programmes changed radically. Funding cuts had a devastating impact on staff morale and the energy available to undertake outside, collaborative ventures. Furthermore, the efficacy of docent programmes as a whole was called into question as paid staff came increasingly to realise the commitment of time and energy required at levels beyond the introductory. At the time, staff members believed that the content of the courses was useful but that it was too much to expect potential or current volunteers to cover the costs of tuition and travel. Current institutional representatives, most often museum educators, believe that it is the responsibility of the institutions themselves or their professional associations to provide training and professional development for both paid and volunteer staff. Of far greater appeal to those interested in the collaborative training of docents is the idea of a regional consortium of museums and galleries. Providers of continuing education within the museum community echo these views (Castle, 1996). The UFT SCS has identified a need; ways of supplying that need are still evolving.

4.6 Issues requiring attention

Each of the volunteer programmes described in the previous sections was set up to meet a perceived need; none was started simply to cut costs. In Chapter Six, we examine some principles of good practice in the management of museum interpretation by volunteers culled from study of these programmes, from study of numerous student tutoring schemes, and from our own pilot programmes in the Science Museum (London). There are, however, some fundamental questions that need to be addressed by anyone thinking of starting a volunteer programme, namely:

1 Why have you decided to have a volunteer programme?
2 What resources of time and talent are within your reach?
3 Who is the programme likely to affect and in what way?
4 What added value (over and above the work of paid staff) does the programme seek to provide and to whom?
5 How much time and money can the museum invest in a volunteer programme?

Possible approaches to these seemingly abstract questions are now illustrated in the particulars of some further case studies.

Pilot volunteer programmes in the Science Museum (London)

From 1994 to 1996, the Nuffield Foundation of the United Kingdom supported a joint project between the Imperial College of Science, Technology and Medicine (Imperial College) and the United Kingdom's National Museum of Science & Industry at the Science Museum (London) (the Science Museum) to study the possible deployment of volunteers in the interpretation and dissemination of science. This chapter reviews what was learned from the pilot projects mounted with Nuffield support.

As indicated previously, the objects of the project were: (a) to develop a programme with volunteer interpreters as a basis for assessing the feasibility of deploying volunteers in the interpretation and dissemination of science and technology in science museums, science centres, and industrial and commercial sites; (b) to help other museums and science centres to set up schemes using models, procedures, and materials generated and tested in the collaborative project between Imperial College and the Science Museum.

The first year was invested in reviewing the current role and management of volunteers and exploring the potential role of volunteers, specifically in museums of science and industry and science centres in the UK and the USA (as reported in Chapter Four). Leading on from this theoretical and field research, new pilot volunteer projects were developed in the Science Museum. These were set up in the light of the case studies, and learning from the successes and failures the first pilot project using student tutors in the Science Museum – the Imperial College/Science Museum Project. Since 1992 this scheme had been experimenting with students acting as museum interpreters/chaperones for schoolchildren.

This chapter describes all of the pilot projects and, through describing how they were set up and how they developed, explains why the decision was made to continue certain pilot projects and suspend others. These pilot studies are intended therefore to reinforce the points made in Chapter Four about the need for schemes to be tuned to local needs and conditions.

5.1 The Imperial College/Science Museum project

In 1992, the British student tutoring scheme, the Pimlico Connection, was extended to involve educational trips to the Science Museum (London) – the Pimlico Connection Science Museum project. The objective was to link the student tutors' classroom-based tutoring to a field trip to the Science Museum.

The Science Museum, the flagship of the National Museum of Science & Industry, is a unique institution. It celebrates an extraordinary story of innovation and achievement. Its collections, without parallel in the fields of science, technology, and medicine, record not only the origins of modern science and industry, but chart human progress from the waterwheel to fibre optics. Fast-changing temporary exhibitions complement the historical galleries by focusing on contemporary science, technology, and medicine.

An extensive programme of events for adults and children including gallery drama, activity workshops, science shows, curator tours and Science Nights (the chance for 8–11 year olds to experience all that the museum has to offer and to sleep among the exhibits overnight) is on offer to visitors throughout the year and enhanced over holiday periods. A selection of resource materials provides support and enrichment for group visits with children of all ages, and a range of teachers' courses provides professional development opportunities particularly for teachers of science, technology, and history. Every year, 1.6 million visitors benefit from the museum experience, a quarter of a million of them coming in educational groups organised by schools, clubs, and societies.

After 17 years of the Pimlico Connection (a student tutoring scheme linking volunteer student tutors from Imperial College to local schools), the Pimlico Connection Science Museum project was created. This new project aimed to link student tutoring with a class visit to the Science Museum, the 'principle being that student tutors, in the classroom and in the museum, could offer the potential to bridge the gap between the visit to the museum and the more normal experiences back at school' (Hughes, 1993).

Pilot project with student tutors 1992/3

From the first year of the Pimlico Connection (1975/6), student tutors from Imperial College had taken the pupils with whom they were working on visits to Imperial College and the Science Museum which is on the adjacent site to the college. However, it was not until the 1992/3 academic year that an attempt was made to use the facilities offered by the museum on a systematic basis.

In October 1992, student tutors who volunteered for the Pimlico Connection classroom-based tutoring scheme were given the opportunity to volunteer for the pilot project. Students were attracted to the project through the student-run Pimlico Connection Society, through posters around campus, and by word-of-mouth personal contact. Student tutors were to be affiliated to certain galleries. The galleries chosen were considered less accessible than most to casual visitors, and student tutors were assigned to one particular gallery through personal choice and availability. Student tutors were then matched to a school that had already booked a visit to that gallery on a Wednesday afternoon.

Five students were selected as museum student tutors, although the interest was far greater. The museum student tutors attended the two-and-a-half-hour mandatory training session on tutoring, along with all the other student tutors. The museum student tutors were then invited to the Science Museum to visit in their own time the gallery to which they had been assigned.

The project was co-ordinated by John Hughes, the then Pimlico Connection Co-ordinator and initiator of the project together with a member of the Science Museum Education Unit staff and a student tutor – the Museum Link Tutor. The Science Museum was the principal contact for the schools and the member of staff was available to answer questions and support tutors when called upon.

Tutors visited the museum on Wednesday afternoons, the time traditionally left free for student sport. Tutors contacted the museum co-ordinator when necessary to ask questions about the gallery and how to interpret it for school-children. The tutors then went into three different schools to assist the teachers with preparing the class for the visit and to assist them to integrate the visit into the normal programme of study. The plan was for the student tutors to spend at least two afternoons in the classroom before visiting the museum. In reality, some student tutors had only one week with the class before the visit.

Qualitative feedback was sought through written questionnaires. The question-naires encouraged respondents to complete sentence-stubs: 'The best thing about the scheme was . . . ', 'The scheme would have been better if . . . ', etc. Feedback from the teachers, the pupils, the student tutors and the museum staff was positive. There was a consensus that the pilot scheme should be expanded. It was apparent that there was a need to focus objectives so that it would become clear *why* the different parties were participating. Specifically, there appeared to be a need for:

- one recognised person to do all external liaison with schools;
- an additional training session at the Science Museum;
- a more detailed evaluation programme.

> It is clear that more detailed support and guidance have to be given to student tutors to reassure them about what they are meant to be supporting in schools; without this they are given a task that they feel is impossible: of trying to become experts on an entire gallery in three Wednesday afternoons.
>
> (Hughes, 1993: 36)

Student tutor volunteers: 1993/4

For the academic year 1993/4, 17 schools and 30 student tutors participated. The recruitment and mandatory tutoring training session was run, as before, by the Pimlico Connection Co-ordinator. Thirty students were assigned to the Science Museum (instead of to a particular school, as was usual in the Pimlico

Connection student tutoring scheme), after attending the training session. Science Museum tutors were affiliated to different schools each term.

On top of the introductory tutoring session, the Science Museum Co-ordinator gave one afternoon briefing session on the practicalities of tutoring in the Science Museum and explained how school teachers booked their classes into the museum galleries and what written resources and gallery programmes were available to support the visit. The student tutors were then assigned to schools in twos and threes. One student tutor who participated in the pilot project the previous year took on the role of co-ordinator for the museum tutors – the Museum Link Tutor.

Schools were attracted to the project in three ways: all schools already working with student tutors were offered museum tutors; schools already booked into the museum on an appropriate Wednesday afternoon were contacted and offered museum tutors; and the museum's *Stop Press* publication made mention of the project (the publication was sent out to teachers and local authorities each term, publicising the term's educational events, and resources and providing a general museum update on new galleries and future developments).

Instead of being affiliated to a specific gallery (as in the previous academic year), student tutors were matched up to a particular school that had requested tutors to assist them with a visit to the museum. The tutors then helped the teacher visit whatever gallery he or she had chosen (frequently outside the student tutor's subject area). As there was more lead time than in the previous year, tutors visited the school one or two Wednesday afternoons before the museum visit, met the schoolchildren in the museum on the afternoon of the visit, and went back into the classroom for one or two afternoons after the visit to follow up on what the children saw and did.

Evaluation questionnaires were circulated to all 30 museum tutors at the end of the academic year and feedback meetings were held with the Museum Link Tutor for the academic year 1993/4 and the new Museum Link Tutor for 1994/5. Evaluation from the academic year 1993/4 was inconclusive, with only nine of the 30 student tutors responding to the questionnaires; no firm conclusions could be made. But some problems and issues were identified. Specifically,

- there was a need for better preparation and training of the student tutors;
- there was a need for better briefing of the teachers receiving student tutors;
- there appeared to be some misunderstanding by the tutors on their role as student tutors.

The first pilot study of the Nuffield-funded project

In the 1994/5 academic year, the Pimlico Connection Science Museum project was developed to incorporate all the recommendations and feedback collected to date. The appointment of a Research Assistant/Volunteer Manager for the project, in early 1994, financed by a Nuffield Foundation grant, allowed a three-fold increase in time commitment from the Science Museum – to approximately two days a week. This meant that more time was available to ensure that both projects were run in parallel with a clear line of responsibility for each project.

The project accepted the first 17 volunteers who stated a preference for the Pimlico Connection Science Museum project rather than the main Pimlico Connection activity, and these volunteers undertook a 15-week classroom-based student tutoring assignment. Those students who opted for the Pimlico Connection Science Museum project committed themselves to eight or 13 Wednesday afternoon sessions – eight in the Winter term and five in the Spring. After the mandatory introductory training session on tutoring, Science Museum tutors were required to attend two additional afternoon training sessions in the museum learning how to enjoy the museum from two perspectives – as a teacher and as a pupil.

Once the training programme was completed, the student tutors were asked to fill out a questionnaire asking about their motivations and expectations of tutoring for the Science Museum. When asked why they chose to participate in the project, students gave varied answers. Many tutors mentioned that they enjoyed the company of children, and explaining science to a younger audience, and that they wanted to spend time in the museum. There were also mentions of student tutoring being directly relevant to course work, specifically for the Communication of Science (undergraduate and postgraduate) courses offered at Imperial College in which some tutors were taking part. Students considered almost unanimously that they would gain 'communication skills' by tutoring: explaining things to schoolchildren would allow them to develop their communication skills while doing something productive. From the students' perspective, student tutoring appears to provide very comparable opportunities to more formal adult education activities (Stedman, 1990).

Students seemed clearly to understand their role as an extra support and unusual resource for the teacher. They believed that tutors might provide or provoke new ideas for teaching and give an opportunity for teachers to try out new classroom projects and to reflect on current ones. They appeared quite modest about what they thought the teacher would gain: 'an extra pair of eyes, ears, and hands', 'enthusiasm'. Only one tutor considered that the teachers might gain 'expert knowledge' from having tutors in the class. Students did appear more idealistic when it came to considering what the school pupils would gain from museum tutors. Most tutors commented on increased one-to-one attention, and there were a number of more ambitious comments such as 'a more thorough understanding of how science is present in the world around us', and 'an insight into science and engineering at university'.

Schools were attracted to the scheme by the same three methods as in the previous year. Only four schools requested museum student tutors in for the Autumn term. Three other schools did put in a request but only after the student tutors had already been assigned to a school. The 17 student tutors were assigned in groups of four and five to the four different schools. Student tutors visited the class for the two afternoons preceding the visit and for two afternoons following, which had not always been possible in the two previous years.

The small number of schools participating in the project for the Autumn term, and the subsequent high student tutor-to-pupil ratio facilitated easier evaluation of the project, by allowing most of the participants to take a more objective view of their work. Comments did, however, indicate that some student tutors thought that their time and energy were not being used effectively or that the teachers felt overwhelmed with tutors in the class.

Feedback lunches were arranged at the end of each term. In both terms, six or seven tutors attended out of a possible 17 and discussed their experience as a tutor while they looked at photos and slides of themselves tutoring on the galleries. A questionnaire similar to that used in the previous year was circulated to all student tutors. The core of the programme of evaluation was self-study involving individual student tutors, co-ordinators and museum staff – following procedures outlined by Kuyper, Hirzy, and Huftden (1993) and by Tremper and Kostin (1993).

In comparison to the previous year's feedback, tutors responded more positively to questions such as 'Do you believe that the school understood why you were accompanying their class to the museum?' and 'Were you clear about what was expected from you as a student tutor?' This may have been a result of the two additional tutor briefing sessions and the increased contact between the schools and the museum through visits and telephone calls by the Science Museum Co-ordinator.

As in previous feedback, the tutors were most enthused by the schoolchildren's reaction to science, the museum, and the effect of their own presence. Tutors were continuously motivated with the knowledge that their presence allowed a whole class to do something different from normal. Answers to the question 'What do you believe the children gained from their visit?' were more positive than in the previous year. In 1993/4 responses tended to be short and vague and stated with not much confidence: 'I think they enjoyed the visit as an activity, and learnt about things that interested them', and 'They were able to see examples of what we had talked about in class. I hope they found the museum an exciting place to be.' In contrast, 1994/5 tutors were more enthusiastic: 'Hopefully a sense that science isn't all about men in white coats. They certainly enjoyed it,' and 'They were so enthusiastic on the day and in the class it was brilliant. They thought it was great to meet real scientists and they all enjoyed the museum and most wanted to come back with their parents.'

The consequence of the increased training and briefing of the tutors and school teachers was more realistic expectations – ones that could be met. However, there were still some doubts from the tutors as to how they could link the museum visit with the classroom experience and whether the teachers planned or even wanted to integrate the museum visit into the course of study or not. Students were definitely more positive in response to the question 'Explain why you believe that you did or did not fulfil what you believe to be the role of a student tutor'. In 1993/4, responses were more matter-of-fact and lacking enthusiasm: 'No connection between visit and class activities,' and 'I felt more was being asked than I gave. I think the teachers had different expectations of me.' By comparison, responses from 1994/5 included such statements as: 'We created work sheets for use in the museum, helped with experiments and due to our knowledge of what was in the museum were able to focus the activities in the classroom,' and 'I do not know if I really have been able to explain science to the children but I know that it was very helpful to have me in the classroom and during the visit to explain and help the children in general.'

Feedback from student tutors indicated that:

- tutors were enthused and motivated by the children's reaction to the museum and the tutors, both on the day of the visit and in class;
- students considered that four tutors were too many for one class of around 25; two or three would be more appropriate;
- students seemed to respond to the increased time commitment from the museum with regard to training and on-going support, and commended the organisation of the project.

Teachers were also asked to provide written feedback on the project; verbal feedback was also given on visits to the schools and by telephone. Teachers were extremely positive on the whole. Three of the seven schools would never have visited the museum had it not been for the student tutors. This was due to the high adult-to-pupil ratio that is stipulated for teachers by the museum and by local government bodies for insurance purposes and practical logistical reasons when on a field trip.

Additional study, particularly of the views of the school pupils, was carried out by Liesbeth de Bakker (1995) using focus group techniques, as advocated by Stewart and Shamdasani (1990). Five of the seven school classes that had taken part in the 1994/5 project took part. The focus group discussions covered the following areas: what the children remembered of the visit, what their expectations were, and whether those expectations were fulfilled. The children were also asked to talk about: the factors that made their visits to the museum worthwhile – or useless and boring; the student tutors and their function; and the amount of science the children learned in the class and in the Science Museum during their visit. The focus group discussions lasted 10 to 25 minutes (with shorter times for pupils from College Park – a school for children with special educational needs); groups were of 6 to 12 pupils. Rather than checking on the acquisition by pupils of specific facts, the research concentrated on the notion advocated by Falk and Dierking that learning 'much more involves the merging and slow incremental growth of existing ideas and information' (1992: 97–8). In particular, the object was to discover if the children's museum experience had been a good one or a bad one.

The focus group discussions indicated that the children had strong memories of their time in the museum over two months after the visits. Many interesting points emerged about what the children learned, and of their very positive appreciation of the students. Perhaps most interesting were the remarks from those children who offered comments about their feelings before and after their visits:

4 thought it would be *boring* and it turned out to be *boring*
11 thought it would be *boring* but it turned out to be *fun*
4 thought it would be *fun* but it turned out to be *boring*
2 thought it would be *fun* and it turned out to be *fun*.

Liesbeth de Bakker concludes that there seemed to be an overall shift to a more positive attitude to the Science Museum from the visits accompanied by student tutors (de Bakker, 1995: 27).

The development of student tutor training techniques.

Experiments were conducted in the development of enhanced training for the student tutors. The usual introductory tutoring session, led by the Pimlico Connection Co-ordinator, presents an insight into classroom tutoring by means of identifying student tutors' motivations and worries about tutoring. The issues raised are then discussed openly. The discussions are led and facilitated by the Pimlico Connection Co-ordinator.

In 1994/5, for the first time in this introductory session, the theory and the practicalities of becoming a Science Museum Tutor were presented to the students by the Science Museum Co-ordinator (Manager of Volunteer Programmes, Stephanie McIvor) and the Museum Link Tutor respectively. The aim was to introduce the idea of a museum experience being a positive and complex learning experience. At the mandatory introductory training session, the Science Museum Co-ordinator presented the more theoretical aspects of the programme: how children can learn and what influences their memories, by focusing on Falk and Dierking's (1992) 'interactive experience model'. This was integrated into discussion by asking the group to share their earliest memory of a museum or field trip with a group, and when it was. Discussion of these experiences (what was remembered and how long ago it was) emphasised to the group the complexities of a museum visit and encouraged the group to consider the impact of a field trip in terms of cognitive and affective learning.

The second session began in Imperial College with a 45-minute talk on the benefits of student tutoring, and an insight into the breadth of its operation around the world, by John Hughes, Project Manager of the BP International Mentoring and Tutoring Project. The Science Museum Tutors were then guided over to the museum for their first hour's induction into the Science Museum. The emphasis of this first training session in the museum was observation of museum visitors and reflection on personal feelings as a visitor. The first 20 minutes were taken up with practical administration details on the location and descriptions of the schools to which the student tutors had been assigned. The following 15 minutes were spent recapping the previous week's ideas on the factors influencing learning in a museum environment and how, as student tutors, they might be able to influence children's agendas and expectations to maximise the benefit of a class visit to the museum. Ideas for this session were drawn from work undertaken by the Association of Science and Technology Centres (ASTC, 1990). The student tutors were then led into the museum to observe visitors and professional museum interpreters – explainers, actors, and guides – at work around the museum.

The final afternoon session looked at methods of presenting science to children by means of questioning children on what they see and observe through comparison, description and recording of their findings. Student tutors were asked to go out into the galleries and look at objects that appealed to them from two perspectives – as both schoolchildren and teachers. They were asked to pick out an object that they believed they would enjoy most as a child, and then another that they believed they would find most beneficial as a teaching resource. Observations from Harlen (1985), Carre and Ovens (1994), and Hayson (1994a and 1994b) were used by the presenter for purposes of comparison. The student tutors then came back to discuss their discoveries with the group and explain what had attracted them to the objects they chose and why they chose them. The only additional written information issued was simple, practical administration details: times, dates, and details of the school visits – together with notes on how to act as a tutor (see Goodlad and Hirst, 1989: Appendix A).

Conclusions drawn from Imperial College Science Museum project

The key to all successful tutoring programmes is *logistics* (cf. Goodlad and Hirst, 1989: 21), with the related advice 'Keep it simple!' In developing this mode of tutoring/interpreting we were aware all along that we were in danger of ignoring our own advice; and so it transpired.

The problem with the project described above is that encountered by most museum educationalists: two different forms of educational strategy and philosophy were operating – that of the schools' curricula concentrating on cognitive learning, and that of the museums – more influential in the affective and psychomotor domains of learning. Also, large numbers of keen but inexperienced tutors were involved. The results were, in retrospect not surprisingly, unsatisfactory.

When asked 'What do you think the schoolchildren gained from your tutoring?', students did not give encouraging responses: they seemed uncertain that their input was valued by the pupils, and the majority questioned the whole worth of a class visit to the museum stating that they thought staying in the classroom would probably be more beneficial than the stress of traipsing to the museum.

Teachers were wholeheartedly in agreement that the project was 'a great idea' in conversations with them leading up to the students visiting the schools. However, feedback collected after the visit and shortly after the last student tutoring session in the school indicated that in more than half the classes the project had not lived up to their expectations.

Although extremely positive feedback was given by teachers, pupils and students in each of the three years (and also in the one term of 1995/6 in which the exercise was repeated), it was clear that the deployment of student tutors as 'volunteer chaperones' was a heavy drain on resources. Looking objectively at the resources required to carry out the project – with regard to the time taken for the teachers and staff from the Science Museum and Imperial College to manage the project, the time given by the tutors tutoring in the school, and the time given by museum staff in training in preparation for tutoring, and weighing this against the varying standards of experience reported by school pupils, student tutors, and teachers, it was decided that the input did not justify the output. It has, therefore, been decided to suspend this particular pilot programme and to look at alternative roles for volunteers throughout the museum. There remains the possibility of going back and redeveloping a museum chaperone project specifically for school groups to museums – again, but possibly in different ways, drawing upon the huge reservoir of talent in Imperial College.

5.2 Researching and developing new volunteer programmes at the Science Museum

The Nuffield funding made it possible to look into matters in a great deal more detail than had been possible previously. In addition to detailed study of the literature on museum interpretation, study of practices and procedures at other museums became possible – in particular with visits to museums in North America that had extensive experience of managing volunteers (see Acknowledgements and the case studies in Chapter Four) It was also possible for one of us (Stephanie McIvor), to undertake detailed consultations within the Science Museum on whose staff she had already worked for two years.

In addition to discussing with all who might have an interest in the matter how best volunteers might be absorbed into the system, she carried out detailed interviews with 12 members of staff from the five different divisions of the museum. These were influential in setting the scene for the additional museum-based pilot programmes described below.

These interviews took the form of informal chats in which Stephanie McIvor began by explaining why she had come to meet them – namely, that she was exploring areas for volunteer deployment throughout the museum as part of a two-and-half-year research and development project for which she needed to find out more about the museum and discover from staff potential areas for volunteer activity. They were invited to talk freely about their initial response to the issue of volunteers in museums and what they considered to be potential areas or duties for volunteers in the Science Museum in relation to their job. They were allowed to think aloud, with only very occasional requests (often signalled only by facial expressions) to clarify points. In short, they were invited to express their personal views on a potentially threatening issue that had become politicised. As an 'inexperienced insider', Stephanie McIvor did not think it appropriate to quiz any staff members on specific issues face to face; rather, they were encouraged to lead the pace, and in many ways the content, of the conversations. Some described their direct and indirect experience of volunteers; each staff member talked quite candidly at a pace and direction with which they felt comfortable. One rigorously went through his sheet of personal objectives and talked Stephanie McIvor through the areas that he considered to be potential areas for volunteers; the majority answered in a very personal subjective way which was exactly what was needed. Nearly all the issues that are explained in an orderly fashion in the volunteer management books were included somewhere in the comments and views expressed by the staff.

The following nine key issues repeatedly came up:

1 *Negative experiences of volunteers* Four of the 12 staff expressed negative views about, or related negative experiences of working with volunteers. One staff member had indirect knowledge of volunteers breaking objects in one museum and stealing whole collections in another. Another had had direct experience of volunteers giving erroneous information about a special exhibition.

2 *Positive experiences/attitudes towards volunteers* Six staff members gave positive examples or anecdotal evidence about volunteers: 'Highly committed resource that will benefit us. Frequently from a different background to the other staff; consequently they could help the Museum to develop in ways that it would like to but doesn't have the knowledge or insight to do so.' 'You can keep volunteers because they want to get something out of what they do compared with some professional paid staff who work mainly for money.'

3 *Worries and concerns about volunteers in the museum or in a particular line of work* Some staff were concerned that other members of staff might find volunteers an intrusion. Others stated that volunteers were obviously very good at offering enthusiasm and time, though they were difficult to manage. One respondent tried to emphasise that the Science Museum was different from other museums and although volunteers were used in comparable lines of work in other organisations, it involved taking risks and the Science Museum could not afford to take such risks.

4 *Time required to manage volunteers* Seven out of the 12 respondents brought up the issue of the time that would need to be invested for volunteers to work productively and effectively.

5 *Procedures required* The most frequently mentioned issue or concern was that of the need to establish a set of procedures and practices. Nine staff provided very practical suggestions, and reassuring comments, about the need for clear procedures and practices on an operational level, i.e., interviewing, security clearance, some kind of agreement or terms and conditions of work, and induction training. 'Organisation is the key to being sure that the use of volunteer staff is going to be effective.'

6 *Quality and standards* Four staff were worried about the risks of dropping standards with regard to the care of the museum's customers, its objects, and its general standards of work.

7 *The future and volunteers* Four staff commented on the long-term prospects for volunteers in the museum and considered that, in the future, the museum would need them, and might not be in a position to discuss the ethical and political issues as practical needs would overshadow such discussions.

8 *Practical suggestions for volunteer jobs* Nearly all staff made practical suggestions as to what volunteers could actually do in the museum. Suggestions included: working with highly skilled members of staff doing

technical work that did not warrant two trained professionals but, for practical reasons, did require two people; deploying volunteers where additional people were likely to provide a better service; creating project work that can be incorporated into a student's course of study. Only one respondent took a much more strategic view, thinking of volunteers as allowing the Museum to extend its field of activities: 'There are plenty of territories untouched.' Many of the comments were substantiated by staff commenting on what specific things they believed would be interesting and motivating for the volunteers to do – working with highly skilled staff members, giving information directly to visitors on the galleries, etc.

9 *The relationship between paid staff and volunteers* Seven members of staff commented on the complex relationship, and differences between, paid and voluntary staff. Two expressed the fear that volunteers would supplant staff as opposed to supporting them. Two staff considered volunteers to be more difficult to manage but for different reasons: one because of the sense of ownership that volunteers tend to have for projects that are entirely volunteer-run, (which was considered to make them more inflexible about taking advice); the other considering that being paid made people more likely to take on one's philosophy and that without payment there was 'no bargaining and no room for negotiation'. Two mentioned the possibility of undermining paid staff's status and skills by encouraging voluntary workers. The need for volunteers to have comparable procedures and practices to paid staff was brought up in two separate interviews: one respondent said 'Organisations that set up volunteers and don't treat them like paid staff fail' – and then listed such things as a comfortable working environment with good facilities, regular feedback from staff, etc.

Staff clearly were aware of the issues at hand but most had had no time before the interview to compose their views and ideas into any kind of cohesive stance. They were all nevertheless acutely aware that the issue of volunteer deployment is complex, having practical, moral, political, and social implications.

The substantial work on volunteer management indicates that many of the concerns voiced by the staff were very astute observations on the risks of managing any staff and in particular volunteer staff, e.g. the concern that the time required to manage the volunteers' work would outweigh the benefit of the work they could do, or the concern to maintain high standards throughout the museum – already a large organisation – when bringing in another new category of staff. Such concerns were, and continue to be, realistic, and should be identified as risks.

However, some the comments by staff indicated assumptions about volunteers in general and specific fears about the management and placement of voluntary staff with the Science Museum, e.g. that volunteers were, by definition, difficult to manage or that volunteers could undermine the status of the staff. It was crucial to the success of the volunteer programme that any such fears should be identified, understood, and allayed. Any museum volunteer programme requires the volunteers to work *with* the staff. We were therefore careful to develop procedures and practices for deploying volunteers that incorporated the suggestions of the staff and responded to their concerns, and chose to formalise regular consultation with staff through a volunteer working group. Staff were thereby involved directly – through the initial interviews, through staff feedback forms on the performance of the volunteers, and through regular meetings of the Volunteer Working Group with representatives from the Trade Union Side and the Museum's Personnel Department. We recommend that any museum planning to introduce a new volunteer programme, or develop a well-established one, should build in some similar consultative initiative.

To address some of the concerns of the staff, and to prepare museum staff for receiving volunteers in their units, Stephanie McIvor provided half-day workshops for museum staff explaining what was proposed, offering the opportunity for further worries to be discussed, and familiarising colleagues with the procedures set out in the appendices to this book, in particular the procedure for recruiting and managing volunteers.

The workshops had the following stated aims:

Practices and procedures

- to provide you with a reasonable working knowledge of the current procedures for deploying a volunteer;
- to enable you to initiate a new volunteer position with confidence.

Management

- to increase your knowledge and understanding of people's motivation to go to work, especially as a volunteer employee;
- to provide you with some new ideas and approaches to management.

The developing role of volunteers in the museum

- To encourage you to enter into the debate on the role of volunteers throughout the museum and to develop well-informed views on the issue.

5.3 National Science Week (events-based)

In 1995 and 1996, volunteers took part in special events at the Science Museum (London) celebrating the National Weeks of Science and Technology, set95 and set96 organised by the British Association for the Advancement of Science. These events invited the public to explore science, engineering and technology by joining in any of over 3,000 events taking place nation-wide at locations from hospitals to railway stations and from schools and universities to museums. Among the events offered by the Science Museum in the week starting 17 March 1995 were the following: a 'star party' in which visitors could hear about the universe and see images from the latest space missions, try their hand at stargazing, see objects in the *Exploration of Space* gallery, meet astronomers, meet an actor playing Apollo astronaut Gene Cernan, and enjoy a fireworks display; BAYSDAYs (British Association Youth Section Days, organised jointly by the Science Museum and Imperial College) which offered a chance to meet Helen Sharman (Britain's first woman astronaut), Professor Heinz Wolff (well known from many television appearances), and Professor Russell Stannard, watch a demonstration of kitchen experiments known as 'exploding custard', take part in a workshop using soap films and mechanical devices to explore mathematics; create fossils from plaster of Paris and make fossil rubbings; design an invention that would improve the way we live and meet inventor Bob Symes to discuss it; see hands-on displays of the latest information and imaging technologies; take part in an Energy Efficiency Day which involved interactive demonstrations on how to cut down on energy use in the home, the chance to see and learn about the gas-guzzling Edsel car, see a drama giving a wry look at the impact of tumble dryers, dishwashers, and other labour-saving devices on energy bills, meet Ann MacGarry from the Centre for Alternative Technology and hear advice on energy saving in the home, take part in a competition to calculate how far one could travel for £10 in various ways – train, car, motorbike, or Apollo 10; take part in a Water Aid Day, hearing how every day 25,000 children die from water-related diseases, hear Pushpa Kapoor (health trainer in India), describe how she tries to promote the use of clean water, and see a drama in which an actor playing the part of Thomas Crapper (Edwardian pioneer of the modern flush toilet) described his contribution to health and sanitation; enjoy an IT and Imaging Weekend in which children and their parents could hear about interactive television, see examples of virtual reality, and see how medical experts, the fire brigade, and crime squads use imaging to diagnose illness, fight fires, and catch criminals.

In set96 (15 March to 24 March), a similar set of activities was offered: the successful 'star party' from 1995 was repeated; Helena Woolley from the Body Shop revealed what went into shampoos; children stood in as planets in a human orrery in a dynamic demonstration by Jack Challoner on how celestial bodies circle each other, asked astronomer Professor Michael Roan-Robinson from Imperial College about black holes, red giants, white dwarves, how stars are born and die; watched museum conservators demonstrating their skills; helped launch water rockets in the Flight Lab; took part in the great egg race; and so on.

In both years, volunteers were recruited to assist paid staff and visiting experts with a wide variety of tasks from simple stewarding – directing visitors around the numerous activities – to assisting with workshops, and stimulating visitors with questions and explanations. The volunteers were sometimes involved in communication and other types of support activities such as playing hosts to guest speakers and assisting with catering. In both years staff were asked how helpful the volunteers had been and the volunteers were asked detailed questions about their experiences.

The volunteers had the following profile: Most were aged between 19 and 34 (19–24: 27 per cent and 25–34: 47 per cent); most (79 per cent) had degrees, with nearly one in five (19 per cent) being postgraduate students. Women out-numbered men (62 per cent women; 38 per cent men).

In 1996, 20 staff (of a possible 30) returned confidential questionnaires. The staff respondents were unanimous in their view that the volunteers had been of help and assistance to visitors, and in saying that they had received no complaints or derogatory comments about the volunteers; they also felt (with only one 'don't know') that the volunteers had been of help and assistance to the staff and/or the guest speakers.

Before working as volunteers, applicants were required to write on a form what their motivation was in applying to be a Science Museum volunteer, and afterwards whether being a volunteer had been a rewarding experience, whether it had been an exciting experience, what they thought their role had been (to check that their instructions had been duly taken on board), how the museum could have helped them more in fulfilling their role, how the museum could have improved the application and selection process, what were the best and worst aspects of their experience, whether they would volunteer again to work in the Science Museum, and whether they would recommend being a Science Museum volunteer to other people. The answers to some of these questions are of domestic interest only (relating to the fine-tuning of internal procedures). However, the answers to the broader questions merit note.

In 1995, 26 volunteers took part, and in 1996, 22. Replies were received from 19 in 1995 and from 18 in 1996, giving response rates of 73 per cent and 82 per cent respectively. In answering the key questions: 'Was being a volunteer a rewarding experience for you?' and 'Would you volunteer to work in the Science Museum again?' all the volunteers said 'Yes' to both.

The most frequently mentioned reasons for applying to be a Science Museum volunteer (number of mentions in brackets) were: wanting to involve others in science by communicating and explaining it (15); being personally interested in science (7); seeing a benefit to his/her professional life (6); seeing a link to his/her studies (3); having time available (3); gaining valuable experience (3); gaining an insight into the Science Museum (2); making productive use of time (2); meeting people/enjoying working with the public (2); undertaking a change in direction (1); and an opportunity to receive training (1).

As indicated, all the volunteers found the experience rewarding. The rewards mentioned included: learning a great deal (9); teaching/educating/involving others (9); helping the public and meeting visitors (9); gaining valuable experience (5); meeting new people (4); being a member of a team (4); gaining an understanding of how the museum works (4); enjoying a complete change from normal work (4); enjoying the feeling of being given responsibility (2); inspiring visitors (2); enjoying a feeling of achievement (2); being welcomed by the staff (1); seeing 'behind the scenes' (1); and gaining confidence (1). The way in which these rewards intermingle is illustrated by the following comment by a volunteer: 'Working with the children on the Design-a-Planet stall gave me a chance to encourage children to be imaginative whilst both they and I had fun.

At the end of the evening, one child protested loudly that she wanted to stay with us learning to draw stars rather than go home. It made me feel very useful.'

In response to a question about the experience being 'exciting', all volunteers made positive statements – but some said that it was fun/challenging/educational, etc. rather than being exciting. Nevertheless, those who had found it exciting made statements about why – many of which again emphasised the learning experience: meeting like-minded people (7); the actual projects and the events (7); learning about new things (6); meeting challenges and demands (5); doing something new/different (5); being a member of a team (4); getting 'hands-on' experience (4); being involved behind the scenes (4); being thrilled to work in a national museum (3); being responsible for knowing and explaining to visitors (2); enjoying the enthusiasm of the visitors, especially the children (3).

Comments about the 'best thing about being a volunteer' tended to reproduce statements that had been made in response to the previous two questions. There were relatively few 'worst thing' comments: some were idiosyncratic (such as 'having to deal with a child who had knelt on a pin'); others mentioned occasionally having to hang around, or missing particular events oneself through being on duty at others.

All the volunteers said that they would like to work in the museum again. Reasons mentioned included the following: it was rewarding/stimulating/fun (19); interest in and experience of communicating science to the public (9); learning about science and/or the museum (7); the feeling of doing something worthwhile (4); liking the atmosphere (3); and being keen on working in museums (2).

Responding to the question 'Would you recommend being a Science Museum volunteer to other people?' none of the volunteers said 'No'. Those who amplified their previous comments mentioned the following points in supporting their enthusiasm: getting experience (volunteer work is about the only way to get experience these days/a chance to evaluate communication skills/gaining new experience) and skills (8); a rewarding experience (6); love of science/interested in contributing to science (6); a rewarding experience (6); enjoyment (5); interest and satisfaction in working in a national institution (3); the chance to go behind the scenes in a famous institution (1); enjoyable, with good people to work with and for (1); other people would also enjoy it/be good at it (1); and the perks were good – free entry to the museum and discounts at the shop (1). The other questions indicated that the volunteers knew what they were supposed to do, valued the training, and thought it appropriate.

In short, the concentrated periods of volunteering, with thorough preparation of the volunteers, not only met the needs and aspirations of the volunteers, but also gave much-needed support to the staff. The nature of the set95 and set96 activities did not make possible detailed assessment of the views of visitors. However, independent research in the Science Museum by the Audit Commission (1991) indicated that asking staff for information was by far the most valued way of getting information in the museum. To this extent, the presence of the volunteers was clearly meeting a need.

5.4 'Information Superhighway' (exhibit-based)

The Science Museum complements its historic galleries with temporary exhibitions. One of the most successful of these has been Science Box – a series of small exhibitions covering contemporary scientific issues (then sponsored by Nuclear Electric). Each small exhibition covers a contemporary scientific subject or issue, and is exhibited in the Science Museum for four months. The exhibition cases were specially designed so that they can be moved around the country to various sites with relative ease as part of the Science Museum On Tour project. They are targeted at the general visitor – non-specialists. The 'Information Superhighway' exhibition was the tenth in the series that opened with 'DNA Fingerprinting' in March 1992. In the last few years the exhibitions have covered such subjects as: nanotechnology (in 'How Small Can We Go?'), the bicycle on which Chris Boardman won a gold medal – 'Superbike', and infertility treatment in 'The Infertility Maze'.

From 29 April to 3 September 1995, the Science Box featured 'The Information Superhighway'. The aims of the exhibition, as set out in the exhibition proposal were to:

- present entertainment, business, education and medical applications of computer networks;
- enable and encourage all visitors to access a variety of graphical, audio and text information;
- survey different sections of the public to discover their attitudes towards 'superhighway' technologies;
- explain how communications networks operate.

The exhibition was built inside three interconnected rooms. The first of these contained: text panels; a video-clip; sections of fibre-optic cable; an Internet simulator; and an interactive 'How Does It Work?' exhibit. The central room, called 'Surf City', contained eight computer terminals where visitors could access the Internet, and volunteer 'Surf City Lifeguards' were on hand to answer questions and help the uninitiated to access and use the Internet. The third room was designed to examine why an 'Information Superhighway' might be needed. It contained interactive exhibits, a touchscreen questionnaire, a video, and text panels.

Forty-five volunteers were recruited, each of whom undertook to give not less than five three-hour sessions over the four-month period under the direction of a temporary, paid co-ordinator. The task of the Lifeguards was to mingle with visitors and help them to use the computers to access the Internet.

An independent evaluation was carried out by Lee Jackson and Sandra Bicknell (Jackson and Bicknell, 1995). Their research revealed that the exhibition's message had been successfully conveyed to the majority of visitors interviewed. A third of interviewees used a computer in 'Surf City' and over a quarter of visitors were observed using a computer during the tracking survey (when visitors were followed and their actions noted in detail). Interestingly, visitors spent, on average, more time in 'Information Superhighway' than in any previous Science Box exhibition. It is not possible to tell whether this was because of the presence of the 'lifeguards' or because the exhibits invited active participation; but several visitors made spontaneous (unprompted) comments on the advantages of having volunteers (the 'Surf City Lifeguards') available to help them (Jackson and Bicknell, 1995: 4. 2. 6(3)).

Additional research was carried out by MSS/Research International Limited (Young and Goulden, 1995) who carried out a 'mystery shoppers' project in the Science Museum during the operation of this project. Thirty evaluators were employed to pass as normal visitors and briefed on what specific aspects of the museum's facilities and services to assess and evaluate – from queue handling at the pay kiosk, through interactions at specific exhibits, visits to the café, toilets, and shop, to walking through and leaving the museum. Comments from these visitors indicated high levels of satisfaction with the service given by the volunteers at 'Surf City': 'Lifeguards were very helpful, polite and well informed', 'The lifeguard was very keen, enthusiastic and helpful', 'The lifeguard was exceptionally helpful and pleasant', 'Lifeguards certainly seemed well informed and in control', and 'She explained things quickly but well'. The only complaints were about insufficient numbers of computers and Lifeguards (suggesting that the exhibition might not have worked at all but for the volunteers) and about the exhibition area being somewhat small, dark, and cluttered. Twenty-nine of the 30 shoppers said that the volunteers had demonstrated to visitors how to log into the Internet; none said that the volunteers could not help at all. (The other respondent said that when they had visited the exhibit, the volunteers had not been able to help because no computers were free.) Detailed comments on the interaction of the volunteers with visitors (greeting them, saying goodbye, etc.) indicated that the volunteers had offered a highly professional level of service.

5.5 Education Unit volunteers

This project was different from all the other pilot volunteer programmes in that volunteers in the Education Unit were asked to carry out specific tasks for a well-defined unit in the museum, rather than being asked to get involved and help out with a broader range of tasks for a time-framed event or exhibition.

All the pilot volunteer projects tend to have been for fixed periods for two principal reasons concerning the staff views about the volunteers and the volunteers' views about volunteering. First, the staff were, and are, concerned that volunteers could pose a threat to paid jobs. In response to this, the majority of volunteers' roles were defined not only by tasks as seen on the job descriptions (see Appendix D) but also by a discrete time frame. Many of our American colleagues had recommended this approach and indeed the massive volunteer programme at the Denver Museum of Natural History (described in Chapter Four) gained in stature and size, and began to have a formal structure, following a special temporary exhibition where it was clear that the role of volunteers was in no way threatening to the core staff and where it also became very apparent that volunteers enhanced the visitors' experience. Second, volunteers are often put off volunteering because of the associated commitment (Lynn and Davies-Smith, 1991). For this reason it was considered that limiting the volunteers' commitment to a pre-determined amount of time might make volunteering more attractive.

Between May 1995 and May 1996, 29 volunteers were deployed as Education Unit helpers. The turnover was higher than had been expected initially but has begun to slow down. In May 1995, the first team of seven Education Unit volunteers was deployed (although all the set95 volunteers were given the opportunity to apply for Education Unit volunteer posts, only two did so – both of whom were accepted).

Education Unit volunteers differed from those on other projects in that they were the first volunteers not supervised directly by Stephanie McIvor. The nature of the work made her supervision both impractical and inappropriate. The first Education Unit volunteers were confined to assisting the four booking office staff with the general administration of, and advisory service given to, the group leaders of the educational groups coming to the Science Museum, which count for over 2,000 free visitors each day throughout the school term. The actual tasks involved were responding to telephone enquiries from teachers and group leaders, sending out written resources and confirmation letters, and generally working under the guidance of the paid full-time and part-time staff.

Volunteers were recruited and trained in the same way as in the previous pilot projects. Interviews were set up to be of benefit to both the volunteers (to brief them on exactly what the job involves) and to the museum (to give the staff a chance to assess if the applicant was suitable for the position). The organisers had taken great care to create a recruitment, training, and management system that encouraged volunteers to voice their views and/or to vote with their feet. The value of this care was borne out in practice. For example, after interview two candidates 'rejected' the museum by choosing not to volunteer.

In September, another five volunteers were recruited. The new tasks and new responsibilities were added to the job. It was thanks to all those volunteers who had played guinea pigs in the first few experimental months of this pilot project that the job has developed into what it is now – that includes those volunteers who left, and those who stayed and had indicated to staff that things could be better and how they could make them so. One volunteer, a retired primary school teacher, had brought to the museum's attention her experience and knowledge of library cataloguing and almost single-handedly re-catalogued the museum's specialist children's library which is used by the Education Unit staff. Another volunteer said that she wanted to have more direct contact with the public. There was clearly a need to expand the volunteers' role in order to make their job more motivating and fulfilling with the aim of decreasing turnover.

A decision was made to offer volunteers the opportunity to work front-of-house over one of the busiest weeks of the year – one of the three school half-term holiday weeks. The number of visitors rises so dramatically over half-term periods that temporary staff are employed through recruitment agencies. It was thought that volunteers would add an extra dimension to the service provided over the half-term period. Volunteers would, through their training and experience, have a far better knowledge of the museum than agency staff and could provide valuable additional information services. Their role was, however, rather ill-defined. Only four volunteers wanted to try working front-of-house. Each was working regular one or two half-day shifts in the week with no volunteer colleagues to hand. After volunteering, three of the four volunteers completed a feedback questionnaire. Although the volunteers found it rewarding and exciting to have worked front-of-house and said that they would take up the opportunity to do so again, comments indicated a degree of uncertainty and discomfort with their role. Two of the three responding volunteers said that the worst thing about being a volunteer was not being kept busy and therefore feeling 'useless' or 'aimless'. When asked at the end if they would like to make further comments, one volunteer suggested that volunteers should work together and support one another; another said categorically that they would like to see the 'front-of-house role extended'.

For the May half-term in 1996, the decision was made not to employ temporary staff through a recruitment agency. The five volunteers then working in the Education Unit were again given the opportunity to work front-of-house, but none of them chose to take up the offer. Consequently, a new team of 11 volunteers was recruited. Instead of working under the supervision of the Volunteer Manager, as volunteers had done the previous October, they were given a better-defined role, and were recruited and trained under the guidance of the professional Explainers on the interactive galleries to assist with visitor flow in and around the most popular galleries. Volunteers wore bright blue sweatshirts with the normal Science Museum logo, and dark trousers or a skirt. Explainers wore emerald-green shirts. The volunteers were stationed outside the interactive galleries where the Explainer team works; their job was to guide and assist visitors to find their way around the museum's galleries and direct them to events or facilities when asked.

The museum was not as busy as on either of the other half terms (October and February). Volunteers worked three to four days, six hours a day, over a period of nine days. The volunteers were, unfortunately, by no means stretched to the limit of their abilities, but working in teams of four under the close supervision of the professional Explainer team, they enjoyed themselves. They were given the freedom to view and participate in the special events going on around the museum, as long as they agreed amongst their volunteer colleagues who was going to remain in the assigned area and ensure that visitors' questions were answered. The volunteers, although they did not feel very stretched, appreciated the realistic expectation that the museum had set for them. Four of the 11 volunteers wrote to Stephanie McIvor personally thanking her for the opportunity to volunteer and enquiring about the prospects for future volunteer work.

After the week, the museum offered all the volunteers the opportunity to volunteer again in other areas of the museum. Seven of the eleven said they wanted to volunteer again and all were successfully placed over the Summer of 1996, fulfilling a variety of tasks in three separate areas of the museum – the Education Unit, the Documentation Centre, and the Science & Society Picture Library.

Stephanie McIvor and the Education Unit staff have been guided by the volunteers into creating a more fulfilling and rewarding position for volunteers, and were not disheartened by the initial high turnover of volunteers. Volunteers were informed on their induction training that they were 'the first intake', and warned of the consequent unavoidable 'risks'. All volunteers were, and still are, actively encouraged from the first day of their training to stop volunteering as and when it stops being enjoyable for them. Although it was requested that they provide feedback as to why they were giving up volunteering, the approach was taken that it was their prerogative to leave, and although the museum staff would like to know, they might not like telling, and were not under any obligation to do so.

The turnover of volunteers has since reduced and is now at a comfortable level – allowing new volunteers to be recruited on a regular but infrequent basis, fitting in with the regular induction training that is run every four/five months.

Episodic volunteering

The successes and failures of the helpers' positions in the Education Unit brings attention to episodic volunteering. Episodic volunteering is defined by Macduff (1991: 1) as (a) volunteering made of separate loosely connected episodes or (b) volunteering of a limited duration of significance to a particular episode. It would appear that the available pool of volunteers coming to the Science Museum is predominantly made up of episodic volunteers. This is not surprising, and indeed it is perhaps a growing phenomenon among volunteers, as people are expected to change jobs more frequently, alternate working and leisure hours, and generally have a more flexible approach to their work. Macduff reports that in an American study by the National Volunteers Centre, it was found that when people who did not volunteer were asked why they were reluctant to do so, 79 per cent said that they would be more inclined to volunteer if jobs were of short duration.

As Macduff says, much volunteer recruitment effort is geared to the regular long-term volunteer, and jobs and training are designed to meet their needs. In the Science Museum, the pilot volunteer programmes have attracted people who want a short, well-defined volunteer position, and those that are looking for a position that can offer them flexibility to offer their time as and when their other personal commitments dictate. The pilot programmes have responded to that need.

Twenty-six volunteers were recruited for set95; five of these volunteers then went on to be Surf City Lifeguards, and two went on to be Education Unit Volunteers. From the 22 volunteers deployed in the set96 project only six were new recruits; seven came from set95, five from set95 Information Super-highway, and four were the Education Unit helpers.

Whilst it is valuable to have experienced volunteers who are familiar with the institution and proficient at the job, the Science Museum has had to recognise that these volunteers are few and far between in Central London, especially when the museum is unable to offer reimbursement of travel expenses. The museum's recruitment strategy and training programme has incorporated and worked with this situation. Volunteer positions for the temporary exhibitions or special events at set95 and set96 were advertised in the national press. Education Unit volunteers are more likely to be recruited from speculative enquiries from people looking for a longer-term assignment.

5.6 Key elements of the pilot programmes

The first and most important aspect of the above pilot projects is the sheer amount of productive time that the presence of volunteers puts at the disposal of the Science Museum (London) and its visitors – see Table 5.1. Excluding the Pimlico Connection Science Museum project (whose beneficiaries were the school pupils at whom the initiative was targeted), and despite the fact that

Table 5.1. Quantitative cost benefit analysis of the Volunteer Programme 1995/6

Event	Hours
National Science Week	
Working	415
Training	130
Total hours given by 26 volunteers	545
Surf City Lifeguards: March to September 1995	
Working	2,000
Training	294
Total hours given by 45 volunteers	2,294
Gallery Researchers	
Working	115
Training	16
Total hours given by two volunteers	131
Education Unit Helpers: May 1995 to December 1995	
Working	360
Training	108
Total hours given by 12 volunteers	468
Total number of hours worked (including tea breaks)	**2,890**
Total number of hours in training	**548**
Total number of hours given by volunteers (including training)*	**3,438**

Note: *This is equivalent to 2.5 full-time equivalents – taking 1,352 hours as the number of actual hours worked by a full-time employee, excluding lunch hours, sick leave and annual leave the Manager of Volunteer Programmes was developing new procedures and working on the Nuffield-funded research (including this book) at the same time, it was nevertheless possible for her to generate activity equivalent to that of 2.5 members of staff. Once a system has bedded down and procedures have been made routine, it should be possible to generate even more (just as the 0.5 FTE appointment of the Pimlico Connection Co-ordinator generates annually some 4,500 hours of student help in schools).

Second, there were indications that the short, sharp, and intensive periods of volunteering suited the volunteers, most of whom had other commitments and were willing and available for only short, defined periods. Third, training of museum staff in how to deploy volunteers was as important as the training of the volunteers themselves – not only to allay their fears (see section 5.2.) but also for the smooth running of the scheme.

These, and other matters regarding the deployment of volunteers in museum interpretation, are addressed more fully in Chapter Six. Meanwhile, Imperial College has now appointed a co-ordinator of the Pimlico Connection on a half-time post and the Science Museum has appointed one of the authors (Stephanie McIvor) as Manager of Volunteer Programmes. Each has wider responsibilities than the project described above – one managing student tutoring by Imperial College students in over a dozen local schools and the other in developing and managing volunteer activities throughout the Science Museum which range from answering questions at special events on the galleries to assisting with the documentation in the Science & Society Picture Library.

6

Some principles of good practice in, and working documents for, the management of museum interpretation by volunteers

The object of this chapter is to offer suggestions that we believe may assist people who wish to set up programmes of museum interpretation by volunteers. In what follows, we confine ourselves to suggestions for the management of museum *interpretation* programmes with volunteers. However, people thinking of setting up volunteer programmes might well wish to read some of the excellent literature on volunteer work in general and the management of volunteers in museums. In previous chapters we have cited some of this literature; but readers may find it useful to look at the following publications on general issues regarding the deployment of volunteers: Adirondack (1992); Conway (1994); Elsdon (1995); Fisher (1986); Graff (1993); Hedley (1991); Hedley and Davis-Smith (1992); Jackson and McNamara (1987); Knapp (1990); Knight (1993); McCurley and Lynch (1994); NCVO (1993); Neate (1995); Rawlings-Jackson and Shaw (1995); Smith (1994); Thomas and Finch (1990); Tremper and Kostin (1993); Volunteer Centre (1990, 1992, 1994a, 1994b, 1994c); Whitcher (1992); Whitcher and McDonough (1992); Wilson (1976); Wilson (1990).

The following give attention specifically to the deployment of volunteers in *museums*: BAFM (1994, 1995); Barbe (1989); Clarke, (1992); Coles (1996); Drake (1986); Ellis (1986, 1990); Fletcher-Brown (1987); Grinder and McCoy (1985); Heaton (1992); Kelly (1986); Kuyper, Hirzy, and Huftalen (1993); Meltzer (1989); Millar (1991); Pinkston (1993); Pitkeathley (1993); Rainbow (1992); Regnier, Gross, and Zimmerman (1992); and Trivulzio (1990).

In the field of the management of museum interpretation by volunteers there are some governing axioms that might be quoted, such as: 'Do not underestimate the capabilities of your volunteers' (i.e. give them genuine responsibility in demanding and interesting activities) – the pilot projects described in Chapter Five support this axiom; 'Do not over-estimate the capabilities of your volunteers' (i.e., do not assume that they can learn in a day what you have learned perhaps over many years; give adequate support through the provision of materials and personal communication) – the feedback we received indicated that our volunteers needed even more briefing than we gave them. Some combinations of duties and tasks we offered to volunteers were too mundane, others were too complex.

There are important similarities between student tutoring/mentoring schemes and museum volunteering involving interpretation that may be represented as follows:

	Student tutoring	*Museum volunteering*
First-hand interpreters	Students	Volunteers (some of whom may be students)
Receivers of first-hand interpretation	School pupils	Museum visitors
Environment in which the interpretation takes place	School of the tutees	Museum
Attending professional communicators (supervisors)	Teachers	Museum staff

We have argued, in Chapter Three above, that much of the research on student tutoring has implications for the planning of museum interpretation by volunteers. Indeed, we have already hinted at the issues that we list below. They are drawn from our study of the literature, discussion with managers of successful volunteer programmes, and the experience (described in Chapter Five) of running different types of volunteer programmes at the Science Museum (London).

There is necessarily a degree of overlap between what follows and the recommendations of Millar (1991) in her study, *Volunteers in Museums and Heritage Organisations: Policy, Planning and Management*, undertaken for the Office of Arts and Libraries (see especially, Millar, 1991: Figure 2). The emphasis we give does, however, reflect our practice-based approach to the subject, describing (primarily North American) examples of good practice, and setting up and learning from successful (and unsuccessful) pilot volunteer projects in the Science Museum (London).

We are assuming in the sections below that the sponsors of a museum volunteer programme will already have thought through the questions that we raised at the end of Chapter Four, namely:

1 Why have you decided to have a volunteer programme?
2 What resources are within your reach?
3 Who is the programme likely to affect and in what way (positively and/or negatively)?
4 What added value (over and above the work of paid staff) does the programme seek to provide and to whom?
5 How much time and money can the museum invest in a volunteer programme?

Once a decision has been taken to proceed, certain issues should be addressed carefully and systematically. These key issues are covered in sections 6.1 to 6.7.

6.1 Define the aims and purposes of involving volunteers in your museum

Having examined available resources and the organisational mission objectives (such as who the programmes are likely to affect and in what ways), explore the ways in which the contribution of the volunteers harmonises with the management plan and organisational structure of the museum. (Appendix C, which is the agreement made in the Science Museum (London) between management and the trade union side on the principles to govern volunteering, is an example of this in practice.) Then write down the aims of the overall programme and the detailed objectives of each part of it.

6.2 Develop clear guidelines about how volunteers will integrate into the current museum management policies

Make sure the staff know precisely what they have to do. This will involve internal lobbying, and careful consultation and communication. It is essential that the staff are involved at this early stage. The staff trust and support of volunteer involvement is of paramount importance. A policy or guidelines should be drawn up to ensure that volunteers will be integrated into the museum and not cause any conflict of interests between staff, the museum management, or visitors. Appendix C is the Agreement drawn up by the Trade Union Side in the Science Museum (London) to protect staff and employees. In a large museum employing hundreds of staff it is customary to have a formalised procedure for involving staff in a way comparable to that used when a new paid position is introduced. Appendix D outlines the six-stage procedure used in the Science Museum (London) for deploying a volunteer.

6.3 Define what the volunteers will do and secure finance

Before volunteers are involved, it is essential to define exactly what kinds of work they will be doing. For some museums, this may be obvious; for others it may not be. Some examples of job descriptions of volunteers are offered in Appendix E. Defining what volunteers will do should then indicate the demands on resources that volunteers will make: specialist advice, training, regular super-vision, access to computers, etc. .

Having written precise job descriptions, calculate the number of volunteers/ volunteer hours needed. Assess the demands to be made on physical space, expenses, the checking in and out of keys, and other administrative procedures necessary to the smooth running of the organisation.

Discuss with museum management where funding is to come from (central budget, appeals, sponsorship). Calculate cost per hour of volunteer time, including the 'overheads' element of the organiser's time, and any 'opportunity costs' in terms of the time of professional staff in helping to train volunteers and/or in inducting them into departmental procedures. The formula for doing this will depend upon local circumstances. For example, in some organisations, the working year is defined as x hours per day for 225 working days – that is, all days excluding weekends, public holidays, and agreed annual leave. The core costs are then the full employment costs of key staff (the manager of volunteer programmes and other museum professionals) including salary, National Insurance, and superannuation, divided by the total number of hours in the working year. To this figure needs to be added appropriate infrastructure costs – heating, lighting, cleaning, building maintenance, depreciation of equipment (computers, etc.). Many organisations use a figure of 80–120 per cent of salaries to calculate this figure. Then figures must be included for any special costs associated with a particular project – uniforms for volunteers, out-of-pocket expenses, advertising, documentation for the volunteers and for the public, and hospitality that will be incurred in supporting the volunteers. Only when all the above things have been attended to should recruitment advertising begin.

6.4 Recruit new volunteers

The methods you use to recruit and train new volunteers will set the ethos of the programme. Think carefully about the skills you are looking for and choose the appropriate advertising media to attract the skills and qualities required: local paper, national paper, colleagues, leaflets or signs used in the museum itself. The better the information you provide for the volunteers, the less selecting you will have to do: to a certain extent, the volunteers will select themselves. It is not enough simply to ask for time to support a cause; you should explain exactly what demands or restrictions will be placed on the volunteer. This may involve an informal chat on the telephone, or a recruitment briefing, or detailed job descriptions and recruitment literature.

6.5 Train and enable the volunteers

As most volunteers work fewer hours than paid staff, it may be more important to provide appropriate induction training and guidance to volunteers than to full-time paid staff before they start work. A basic induction programme can be given as a formal training session or as on-the-job guidance – familiarising the volunteers with the aims of the museum, its history and development, and some practical information on how to conduct themselves in the museum. Whichever way it is delivered, we recommend that some record of induction is maintained to ensure that all new volunteers are provided with appropriate guidance to enable them to do the job for which they have been recruited. Appendix G offers a template used in the Science Museum (London) for a half-day formal training course; Appendix G also provides extracts from the *Volunteers' Handbook,* and a practical introduction to the formal Volunteer Agreement.

It is beneficial to involve as many volunteer supervisors as possible in the induction training – these can be members of staff or fellow, more-experienced volunteers. This emphasises to volunteers that they are working under the guidance of the experienced museum personnel, and gives staff the opportunity to set standards and guidelines for the volunteers' behaviour.

6.6 Motivate and support the volunteers

The needs of volunteers are met by providing the volunteers with the conditions that will motivate them – a complex balance of the intrinsic and the extrinsic. By definition, the more complex motivation is likely to be intrinsic – which requires designing a volunteer's job that is useful and makes the volunteer feel valued. Extrinsic motivators (including such benefits as shop discounts, free entry for family and friends, car parking facilities, etc.) may make the volunteer feel more valued but are unlikely to change a volunteer's decision as to whether to continue volunteering or not. Meaningful work is more likely to be significant to the volunteer than tangible staff benefits. Volunteers' jobs will also need to be updated and refined constantly to reflect the needs of the museum, the staff, and the individual.

6.7 Develop the volunteer programme through feedback from visitors, staff, and the volunteers themselves

Seek feedback from visitors, staff, and volunteers on a regular basis – either through informal personal chats or through more formalised but confidential questionnaires. The most telling feedback has proved to be from volunteers who have recently stopped volunteering or staff who no longer want to work with volunteers. It is valuable to stress the importance of feedback at the start of the recruitment exercise.

Feedback is only as good as what you do with it. If it is not possible to respond to suggestions, it is essential to explain to staff and/or volunteers why it is impossible. Explain the restrictions under which you are operating and why you may not be able to respond to all suggestions.

Fundamental to the whole process of volunteering is the management task of balancing the interests of the paid staff, the museum management, the visiting public, and the volunteers themselves. None must be short-changed.

6.8 Concluding observations on the management of museum volunteers

Volunteering is a co-operative human activity. It requires the active involvement of givers and receivers. Both the museum and the volunteer should be seen as giving and receiving time, experiences and opportunities. It is both necessary and desirable to give equal consideration and attention to the volunteer as a resource and as an audience (see Martin, 1994).

Volunteers as an audience

Volunteers are recipients of enjoyable experiences. These include opportunities to learn, to meet other people, and to assist others. They are a special adult client group that museums serve. Few museums allocate a great deal of time to the provision of adult education in comparison to other aspects of education work (Chadwick and Stannett, 1995). Yet trends indicate a growing demand for adult education by the year 2000, with an increasing number of older people, and more educated museum visitors (see Middleton, 1991). Our research indicates that museum volunteers find their work rewarding because they are offered a learning experience.

Volunteers as a resource

Museums are recipients of volunteers' time, a gift which has unique qualities but also incurs costs. The intrinsic motivations of volunteers have been shown to relate to a high quality of service for clients (Neate, 1995). This quality of service is difficult to surpass and an invaluable, unique asset to museums as they compete with profit-centred leisure industries. However, individuals, whatever their level of commitment, need to be recruited, trained, and guided – which takes time and therefore costs money. Lack of management of volunteers in the past has often been based on the false assumption that volunteer time is unlimited and free. In fact, it is neither, and therefore needs to be carefully managed. Managing volunteers involves balancing the 'gifts' exchanged between the museum and the volunteer. Volunteer managers must first identify the gifts that can and should be exchanged. In order to do this we should think about what motivates the individual to volunteer and, in addition, what motivates the museum to deploy volunteers. This will give us an idea of the expectations one holds of the other. In other words, we need to consider what each party wants to receive, and what each party is willing to give.

People volunteer in museums:

- to satisfy personal aims;
- because they identify with and wish to support the aims of the museum;
- because their actions can have a positive effect on other individuals.

Museums deploy volunteers because they can:

- provide a high-quality service;
- facilitate new experimental projects that are outside the museum's core objectives;
- offer specialist skills to augment those of salaried staff;
- expand the museum's services to serve more visitors;
- act as visitors' advocates, providing a direct link into the community.

In a successful volunteers' programme a balance of the above expectations is met for both sides. Unbalanced exchanges result in exploitation by one party or another, which inevitably leads to conflict. Unfortunately, there is no easy formula for achieving a fair balance of gifts. However, we suggest that the answers to the following questions may help museums to develop a structure for a progressive volunteer programme.

Volunteer Managers should ask themselves:

1 What are the expectations of the volunteer programme from the perspective of the museum and the volunteers?
2 What are the costs and benefits of meeting these expectations?
3 What are the principal aims of deploying volunteers?

We should be thinking of museum volunteers as both a resource and a client group. They give and receive gifts in the form of time, experience, and opportunities. Good volunteer management ensures that volunteering is mutually beneficial for both the museum and the volunteer. The key to a good volunteer programme is thinking strategically about how to combine the volunteers' dual role as a resource and an audience.

Appendix A

Origins and developments of student tutoring

Bell and Lancaster

Many teachers in different times and places have used some form or other of student tutoring to reduce the stress of dealing with large classes. We know, for example, that monitors were employed in Elizabethan grammar schools in England (Seaborne, 1966). However, credit for the first systematic use of tutoring must go to Andrew Bell (born 27 March 1753) and Joseph Lancaster (born 25 November 1778) (see Goodlad and Hirst, 1989: 23–6).

In 1789, Andrew Bell was appointed Superintendent of the Military Male Asylum at Egmore and Minister of St Mary's Church at Madras. The asylum was a semi-official charity school for the orphaned boys of soldiers. Walking on the beach one day, he saw children drawing in the sand; this gave him the inspiration of using trays of sand as a cheap teaching resource. Having failed to enthuse his teaching staff with the idea, he started, in 1791 or 1792, to use children to teach other children with the trays. He soon realised that this use of monitors was an educational discovery far more important than trays of sand. He wrote up his work for the directors of the asylum, publishing in October 1797 his *Experiment in Education*. Salmon (1932) has reproduced the practical parts of this work, along with sections of the *Improvements* of Joseph Lancaster – another early pioneer.

Joseph Lancaster opened his first school at the age of 20 in 1798. He was particularly interested in providing education for children who would not otherwise get it. In June 1801, he moved into a room to accommodate 350 boys in Belvedere Place, Borough Road, London. Three hundred and fifty pupils were too many for him to teach alone; accordingly, he started to use boys who knew a little to instruct those who knew even less. He acknowledges his debt to Andrew Bell, whom he met in 1804 when Bell was back in England as rector of Swanage. Perhaps because he was a more flamboyant publicist, Joseph Lancaster succeeded in raising considerable sums of money from the nobility as subscriptions for his schools. Unfortunately, Lancaster's style of spending was as flamboyant as his fundraising and publicity; he was, in fact, arrested for debt in 1807. Nevertheless, his ideas had a certain currency in America and in England until they fell into disuse with the growth from the 1840s onwards of the profession of trained full-time teachers.

The foundations are laid: research on tutoring

In the 1960s in the USA, many tutoring schemes were developed to meet situations of acute need, often in inner-city areas. Some of the best-known were the 'Youth Tutoring Youth' programme of the National Commission on Resources for Youth Inc.; the New York High School Homework Helper Programme; and the Tutorial Community Project, Pacoima, California (see Goodlad and Hirst, 1989: 37–42).

A variety of theories inform the different forms of practice of deploying non-professionals, particularly young people, to help to teach others. For example, role-model theory suggests that tutor's behaviour will be constrained by what those who are tutored (tutees for short) expect of a teacher, and that the tutors will thereby come to sympathise with the teacher. Tutees are more likely to learn from their peers than from their teachers, who may be perceived as coming from an alien world. Behaviourist theory asserts that learning will be efficient if every correct response to a question by a pupil is rewarded, the reward acting as a stimulus to make another step in learning. Tutoring can offer rapid reinforcement of learning. Socio-linguistic theory stresses the effect of social upbringing on patterns of speech and therefore of perception. Tutoring offers pupils practice in speech codes with which they may be unfamiliar. Gestalt theory asserts that learning will occur when the learner 'locates' an item in an intellectual structure. Tutors have to reflect on what they have learned in order to be able to represent it to their tutees and thereby master it better.

Translated into hoped-for benefits for tutors and tutees respectively are the following expectations.

Tutors should benefit from taking part in tutoring by:

- developing their sense of personal adequacy (role-theory);
- finding a meaningful use of the subject-matter of their studies (Gestalt theory);
- reinforcing their knowledge of fundamentals (Gestalt theory);
- experiencing being productive (role theory);
- developing insight into the teaching/learning process (Gestalt theory).

Tutees should benefit from being tutored by:

- receiving individualised instruction (behaviourist theory);
- receiving more teaching than in a conventional class (behaviourist theory);
- responding to their peers (role theory and Gestalt theory);
- receiving companionship from tutors (Gestalt theory).

The work of the pioneers began to attract serious attention when a number of closely controlled studies revealed striking benefits from tutoring such as the following:

- 16-year-old schoolchildren improved their own reading skills by tutoring younger children (Cloward, 1967);
- tutoring given to children by students was more effective than an equal amount of normal classroom instruction (Klosterman, 1970);
- the improved verbal skills of tutored pupils persisted over two years (Shaver and Nuhn, 1971);
- hour-for-hour, mathematics tutoring by students was as effective as teaching by trained teachers (Bausell, Moody, and Walzl, 1972).

Cognitive gains of this type have consistently been easier to demonstrate than affective gains; although there are numerous qualitative accounts of the beneficial effects of being a tutor or a tutee on self-esteem and behaviour, there are relatively few psychometric studies demonstrating these effects. Goodlad and Hirst (1989: Chapter Four) and (1990: Chapter One) give a comprehensive account of research findings on the outcomes of tutoring activities, including: the effect of pairings of tutors and tutees by age, sex, ability/achievement, and social background; the number and duration of sessions; the number of tutees per tutor; the training of the tutors; and structured versus unstructured tutoring – i.e., tutoring following very closely defined guidelines compared with that in which tutors can develop the interaction as they please. Topping and Hill (1995) give further information about the range of tutoring schemes on a number of dimensions: tutee characteristics; tutor characteristics; curriculum; contact constellation; time; place; style; goals and outcomes for tutees; goals and outcomes for tutors; and explicit rewards for tutors. For those seeking further information, Allen (1976), Kalfus (1984), and Klaus (1975) give critical reviews of early research in the field. Feldman, Devin-Sheehan, and Allen (1976) and Paolitto (1976) discuss some of the methodological problems involved. Wilkes (1975) offers a comprehensive, annotated bibliography on peer- and cross-age tutoring and related topics up to 1975. Cohen, Kulik, and Kulik (1982) offer a meta-analysis of research (i.e., statistical analysis of the large collection of results from individual studies for the purpose of integrating the findings).

The type of tutoring that has, perhaps, the greatest similarity to museum first-person interpretation is tutoring by university students of school pupils. Schemes involving university students as tutors now operate on a massive scale. Probably the largest single scheme is the PERACH project in Israel which deploys more than 12,000 tutors each year (Fresko and Carmeli, 1990). Initiated on a small scale in 1974, PERACH arranges for students to tutor needy children all over Israel. Most tutoring is conducted on an individual basis: tutor and tutee meet twice weekly in two-hour sessions over the course of an academic school year. The tutors are not simply private instructors, but are expected to stimulate a desire to learn, to reinforce self-confidence, and to broaden the tutee's base of general knowledge and experience. Some group tutoring exists as well in which the emphasis is more academic than personal. PERACH also sponsors a number of enrichment programmes in the areas of health, sports, nature, and the arts, through which university students can apply their particular interests and skills for the benefit of disadvantaged children. As compensation for their activity, all tutors are awarded a partial rebate of their university tuition fees. The scheme has been subjected to regular research – on the scheme as a whole (PERACH Central Office, 1984), as to the effects on the tutees (Eisenberg, Fresko, and Carmeli, 1980a, 1980b, 1981, 1982, 1983a, 1983b) and more recently on the tutors (Fresko and Eisenberg, 1985; Fresko, 1988; Fresko and Chen, 1989). The activity has been shown to be effective in motivating children and beneficial to the tutors.

In the USA, two major studies, sponsored by the US Department of Education, revealed the massive scale of activity there (Cahalan and Farris, 1990; Reisner, Petry, and Armitage, 1990). Cahalan and Farris (1990) found that college-sponsored programmes involving college students tutoring or mentoring elementary and secondary school pupils were being implemented in slightly under one-third (29 per cent) of all two- and four-year colleges and universities. Out of the total of 3,212 institutions studied, 921 sponsored at least one programme; some had more than one programme, with an estimated 1,700 programmes nationally. In two-thirds of these programmes, the primary focus was tutoring, with mentoring taking place in 17 per cent of them. The remaining 16 per cent, although involving tutoring and mentoring, had some other 'primary focus', such as diagnostic evaluation and respite care. In the academic year 1987/8, some 71,000 college students were serving 240,000 elementary and secondary students.

The complementary study by Reisner, Petry, and Armitage (1990), examining the same set of programmes and projects, reports that they had positive effects on: the test scores, grades, and overall academic performance of disadvantaged elementary and secondary students; their motivation and attitude towards education; their familiarity with environments other than their own; and their self-esteem and self-confidence. They also report that taking part in tutoring and mentoring projects helps students to: obtain practical experience and improve their leadership and communication skills; develop a greater commitment to community service; and increase their self-confidence and self-esteem. The authors note that successful projects tend to include the following:

- defined time-commitments from tutors and mentors;
- systematic screening of prospective tutors and mentors and matching with younger students;
- thorough training and monitoring of tutors and mentors;
- close relations between the sponsoring colleges and participating school systems.

The scheme of student tutoring at the Imperial College of Science, Technology and Medicine described in Chapter Three has become the model for some 180 similar schemes in the United Kingdom and many overseas. (Details of many schemes are offered in note form in Appendix B of *Students as Tutors and*

Mentors (Goodlad, 1995a). See also Jones 1989, 1990, 1993a and 1993b.) Currently, some 200,000 young people world-wide are receiving tutoring from students through schemes modelled on the Pimlico Connection. Because the scheme has been thoroughly researched over a period of 20 years, and because the findings are highly relevant to the field of museum interpretation by volunteers, it is described briefly here.

Appendix B

Manager of Volunteer Programmes – an aide memoire

These notes describe the work of the Manager of Volunteer Programmes at the Science Museum. They are intended as an aide memoire to the present post holder (Stephanie McIvor) and a potential guide to any successor and/or assistant. They may also be of value to people working in other museums.

Aims and objectives of the Science Museum's Volunteer Programme

For the museum

- To increase the quality of service that we provide to all our visitors, without incurring the additional cost of paid staff.
- To provide a vehicle for broadening the museum's visitor profile, and to attract a more representative sector of the public into the museum.

For the visitor

- To enhance the visitor experience at the museum by adding services which financial constraints would otherwise prohibit.

For the volunteer

- To provide an opportunity for 16–75 year olds to learn about the museum and gain new skills and experiences.
- To allow the public to participate in, and actively contribute to, the Science Museum's work in an area of personal interest.
- To offer a structured training programme for all volunteer staff.

For the staff

- To provide a supplementary work force.
- To release museum staff to undertake more specialised work of greater value.

Duties of the Manager of Volunteer Programmes

- Designing volunteer jobs.
- Formulating the recruitment policy.
- Establishing and running the volunteer database.
- Organising the delivery of training for volunteers.
- Training paid staff with whom volunteers will be working.
- Establishing and managing the supervision and appraisal procedures for volunteers.
- Organising and co-ordinating volunteer support and development, e.g. access to facilities, newsletters, discounts and, where needed, advice on career paths.
- Liaising with Personnel Services.

Appendix C

Science Museum agreement with Trade Union Side, January 1993

General Principles

- Volunteers will be professionally recruited and trained.
- Volunteers will be issued with a contract and be subject to appropriate personnel procedures.
- A volunteer co-ordinator at each museum (the Head of Personnel & Training at the Science Museum) will oversee and co-ordinate the contributions of all volunteers.
- They will supplement rather than supplant the work of existing staff but will be engaged on real work that budgetary constraints would otherwise prevent the museum from discharging.
- They will be professionally guided, managed and controlled by appropriate full-time employees who will be responsible for their outputs as they are for other groups of staff.
- They will be rewarded by such modest concessions as are felt to be reasonable e.g. catering and retail concessions, tokens of recognition (badges, ties?) for long and satisfactory service. Whilst volunteers would normally be expected to bear their own travel costs some out-of-pocket expenses may be reimbursed at local discretion in exceptional cases.
- Volunteers should be appropriately qualified with documentary evidence of specific skills supplied in appropriate cases. Tasks on which volunteers work will be specific and time-bounded (i.e. they will work on defined tasks the need for which would be subject to prior assessment by the line manager concerned).
- The health and safety of volunteers and museum staff and the security of museum objects will be appropriately safeguarded (e.g. volunteers will receive appropriate training in health & safety matters, will not have access to dangerous equipment unless properly supervised, and will be subject to the usual health declaration procedures etc.).
- The museum will provide adequate accommodation and equipment.
- Volunteers will not be given work of such a nature as to deprive full-time staff of any component of their work which compromises their career development or job satisfaction.

- Trade Union Side (TUS) will be consulted when proposals are made to use volunteers in new capacities through the medium of a standing working party consisting of delegated TUS representatives and management, including the volunteer co-ordinator.
- Volunteers will normally work a maximum of seven weeks in a calendar year, preferably as one day per week; in some cases volunteers could work more frequently for a defined shorter period.

Additional Guidelines

- Volunteers will be able to include voluntary service on their CVs; where requested the museum will supply a reference.
- All volunteers will receive general induction training; specific on-the-job training will be delivered by the appropriate line manager.
- In due course, a handbook for volunteers will be produced setting out all the arrangements appropriate to volunteers in NMSI. This will be subject to appropriate local variation for the Science Museum, National Railway Museum and the National Museum of Photography, Film & Television.
- TUS will have access to museum managers locally and the Head of Personnel & Training (in the case of the Science Museum) on any matter concerning volunteers about which they have specific concerns.

Appendix D

Volunteer deployment: The procedure, questions & answers and volunteer forms

The six stage procedure

1 Formally initiate a request for a volunteer

Complete a 'Volunteer Request Form' and send it to the Manager of Volunteer Programmes.

2 Write a job description for the new volunteer position

Discuss the propsed new volunteer position with the Manager of Volunteer Programmes and create a draft job description.

3 Propose the new volunteer position to the Volunteer Working Group

Present the draft job description to the Volunteer Working Group. The members of this group are: a representative from Personnel Services, the Manager of Volunteer Programmes and a representative from the TUS.

4 Advertise the new position

The Manager of Volunteer Programmes will circulate the details of the new position to all past volunteer applicants.

If the new position requires a large team of volunteers or requires very specific and specialised skills, it can be advertised in the national press or circulated to target groups through a mail shot.

5 Recruit and select the volunteer

Select volunteer(s) on the bases of their application form and a 30 minute informal interview. The Manager of Volunteer Programmes arranges the interviews.

6 Train and manage the volunteer

The Manager of Volunteer programmes arranges and administers the induction training.

The supervisor of the new position must ensure that the volunteer is provided with specialist training, on-going supervision and appropriate management support.

Questions and answers

How much time will it take me to recruit a volunteer?

Stage 1, 2 and 3 should each take **you** no longer than 45 minutes each. Stage 4 does not involve you. The length of time required for stage 5 and 6 will depend on the number of applications received for the position and the number of volunteers that you are looking to recruit.

How long will the process take from the time I complete the 'Volunteer Request Form'?

The time line shown below illustrates the process at a very 'easy going' pace. It is possible to complete the process in a couple of weeks. The speed of the process will be dictated by the kind of position proposed. If the position is in a new area where volunteers have not previously worked it will probably need the full 10 weeks.

WEEK 1	WEEK 2	WEEK 3	WEEK 4	WEEK 5	WEEK 6	WEEK 7	WEEK 8	WEEK 9	WEEK 10
complete request form	draft a job description	discuss with volunteer working group			receive applications			interview applicants	train new volunteers
			advertise and circulate job description			arrange interviews			

How much time should I set aside for a volunteer?

Once you have deployed a volunteer it is your responsibility to supervise and manage that person. The specific position that the volunteer holds will dictate how much planning, supervision and management this demands.

So what does the Manager of Volunteer Programmes do?

The Manager of Volunteer Programmes facilitates the process of deploying volunteers in the museum. He/she has a thorough knowledge of the legal, theoretical and practical aspects of recruiting, selecting and managing volunteers.

He/she: advises on whether a proposed volunteer position is viable; assists staff to create new volunteer job descriptions; chairs Volunteer Working Group meetings; arranges and plans the publicity of new volunteer positions; sends out volunteer information packs to new applicants; and responds to all incoming application forms and enquiries about voluntary work.

He/she also arranges induction training for new volunteers; organises social events; and produces a regular Volunteers' Newsletter.

Volunteer request form

Request initiated by .... Extension number ....

Summary of project

Describe the project or area of work for which you are looking for voluntary assistance

---

Tasks and duties to be performed by volunteers

List principal tasks to be completed by volunteers

Reason for requesting voluntary assistance as opposed to employing paid staff ?

Time scale of project Circle/complete as appropriate

Does the project have a finite end? **Yes No**

If yes, how many days should it take to complete the tasks listed above? ...... **days**

If the project has a fixed time scale please state the start and end dates of project

.... / .... / .... — .... / .... / ....

Number of volunteers requested (Volunteers work an average of four hours each week)

How many volunteers had you considered working with at any one time ...... **volunteers**

How many volunteers had you considered working with in total ...... **volunteers**

When would you like the volunteer(s) to start work ..... / ..... / .....

Supervision of volunteer

Who will be responsible for supervising the volunteers and monitoring their hours and performance?

Name a principal supervisor and a deputy to act in his/her absence

name.. *signature*..

name.. *signature*..

Training of volunteer

Who will be responsible for ensuring that volunteers are appropriately trained?

name.. *signature*..

Volunteer job description form

		Details of proposed new volunteer position
What will the volunteer do?	List all the tasks	
How?	State the experience required/preferred	
	List the skills required/preferred	
	List the personal qualities required/preferred	
	Describe the training that will need to be provided	
When?	Stipulate working hours	
Where?	State location of work	
With whom?	State who will be working with the volunteer(s)	
Reward/ Remuneration	Describe any rewards that you envisage the volunteers will receive, i.e. training, experience.	

Appendix E.1

Briefing for student museum chaperones

What is the difference between The Pimlico Connection Student Tutoring Project and The Science Museum Chaperone Project?

The Science Museum project has been set up to operate on the same principle as the main Pimlico Connection project. It aims to be mutually beneficial to everyone involved: you as the tutor, the pupils that you will be tutoring and the teacher that you will be supporting. The Science Museum project differs only in that it has a slightly different emphasis. Instead of concentrating on enhancing classroom based activities, your tutoring will focus on making the most of a visit to the Science Museum.

What is the point in focusing on a museum visit as opposed to classroom based activities?

We believe that museum visits can provide an excellent environment for enhancing and re-enforcing classroom based courses of study. But museum visits are time consuming and expensive. It is, therefore, important to try and maximise the benefit of a class visit to a museum.

Why involve Student Tutors in a museum visit?

Most of the classes you will be assisting would not visit the Science Museum without your support. The Science Museum offers free admission to all educational parties visiting on week days throughout the school term but this still excludes many less privileged schools. This is because field trips are very demanding on resources and many schools may not have:

- the financial resources to arrange a private bus to the museum,
- the staff resources or parental support that is required to chaperone a class on a museum visit,
- the staff time that permits the teacher to make a pre-visit to the museum and thoroughly plan the aims of the visit and associated classroom activities.

You may be able to help teachers and pupils visit the museum by assisting them to overcome these barriers.

How will the school pupils benefit?

A museum is an unusual and intensive learning environment; it can be very influential not simply on a particular course of study but on pupils' whole approach towards learning and discovery. You cannot and should not judge the significance and benefit of your tutoring simply by the number of facts that the pupils remember or concepts that they can explain. A museum visit can have a greater and more lasting effect in many less intangible ways.

Appendix E.2

Volunteer job description

Department   Education and Programmes Unit

Project   **set96 – National Science Week 15 to 24 March 1996**
set96 is a national celebration of science, engineering and technology.
Volunteers will assist staff in running the exciting programme of visitor events throughout National Science Week.

Title   **set96 Events Assistant**

Event times   Friday 15 March & Saturday 16 March: 09.30–16.00
Sunday 17 March: 09.30–17.30
Friday 22 March: 17.00–22.00
Saturday 23 March: 09.00–17.00
Sunday 24 March: 10.00–17.30

Reports to   set96 Manager

Responsibility   To attend briefing and training sessions.
To assist staff to set up and prepare for events for the set96 events programme. To be pro-active in assisting visitors to orientate themselves in the museum and find set96 events. To work as a team with staff and volunteers.

Tasks
- Assisting staff to prepare and set up events.
- Staffing activity areas for two-hour shifts.
- Encouraging visitors to explore and enjoy the set96 activities.
- Providing visitors with information on the entire set96 programme.
- Advising visitors on other museum programmes and services.

Requirements
- An ability to communicate clearly to the public.
- An enthusiasm to explain science to other visitors.
- The ability to work as part of a team and support other volunteers.
- A commitment to work to an agreed timetable.
- Confidence to be proactive in explaining the activity assigned.
- An ability to work independently.
- A friendly and courteous manner.
- A basic scientific background would be an advantage.

Training   Half day general museum induction course including a brief history of the Museum and the front of house code of practice. Specialist training on the assigned activity prior to shift.

The National Museum of Science & Industry is an equal opportunities employer.

Volunteer job description

Department	Education and Programmes Unit
Title	**Education Helper**
Available Shifts	Monday to Friday: 09.30–13.30 and 13.00–17.00 Minimum commitment of three shifts per month. Maximum of 15 shifts in any three-month period.
Reports to	Education Managers and Education Assistants
Responsibility	To assist the Education Booking Office accept and process school bookings, and to send out resources to schools. To help Education staff research and develop new written resources. To help staff co-ordinate and run educational events.

Tasks or Current Projects

- Assisting the Education Booking Office to answer teachers' enquiries, send out educational resources and process school bookings.
- Joining a team of staff and volunteers who answer project enquiries from pupils and teachers.
- Researching popular science topics to help write information leaflets that will be used in response to the project enquiries.
- Reviewing the field of educational publications in order to develop and update a database of contacts for marketing purposes.
- Researching a list of schools/colleges who are connected to or interested in the Internet.
- Meeting and greeting school groups that have booked for Education workshops and events.

Requirements (depending on the projects in which you participate)

- An interest in education and learning in museums.
- An ability to communicate clearly and courteously on the telephone.
- The ability to work as part of a team and support staff and volunteers.
- A careful and rigorous approach to research.
- An interest in writing educational material.
- Some experience or interest in the Internet.
- General office administration skills would be an advantage.

Training

Full day general museum induction course including Front of House Code of Practice and an introduction to education in the Science Museum. Specialist on the job training.

The National Museum of Science & Industry is an equal opportunities employer.

Volunteer job description

Department   Exhibitions Unit

Project   **Information Superhighway – a Science Box Exhibition**
Science Box is a series of temporary exhibitions focusing on
contemporary science. The Exhibition will be open from 26 April
to 3 September 1995. A team of volunteers will work on the
exhibition assisting visitors to access and use – 'surf' – the
internet. Up to three volunteers may be required for each shift.

Title   **Surf City Lifeguard**

Available Shifts Monday to Sunday: 09.45–14.00 and 13.30–18.00
Minimum commitment of three shifts per month.
Maximum of 15 shifts in any three month period.

Reports to   Chief Lifeguard

Responsibility To work with the Chief Lifeguard and assist him/her in helping
visitors to access the Internet. To be pro-active in ensuring that
visitors have a positive experience of the Internet.

Tasks
- Welcoming visitors to the exhibition.
- Issuing tickets for the exhibition at busy times.
- Encouraging the visitors to 'surf' the Internet at the exhibition.
- Explaining the internet to visitors.
- Helping with other Front of House services such as ushering
  and general information throughout the museum.

Requirements
- An ability to communicate clearly and effectively with the
  public.
- The ability to work as part of a team and support other
  volunteers.
- A commitment to working to an agreed timetable.
- An ability to work with visitors of all ages.
- A friendly and courteous manner.
- A proven interest in the Internet or an interest in learning more
  about the Internet.

Training   Full day general museum induction course including Front of
House Code of Practice and specialist Internet training. Extra
retraining workshops once a month.

The National Museum of Science & Industry is an equal opportunities employer.

Volunteer job description

Department	Research Unit
Title	**Volunteer Visitor Research Assistant**
Available Shifts	Monday to Friday: 10.30–13.30 or 12.30–15.30
	Minimum commitment of approximately 25 hours each month for 4 months (two shifts every week).
Reports to	Senior Researcher
Responsibility	To attend relevant training sessions and assist the Research Unit staff collect and process data. To follow the Research Unit's ethical practices in social science, and the National Museum of Science & Industry's Front of House Code of Practice. To work as part of a team with museum staff and keep the Senior Researcher informed as to when the work will be carried out.

Tasks

- Interviewing and observing visitors.
- Processing data, collating visitors' responses, calculating relevant statistics, drafting outline reports.

Requirements

- A willingness to approach and interview Science Museum visitors aged 2 years and upwards.
- The ability to work as part of a team comprising of Science Museum staff, other volunteers and contract workers.
- An ability and willingness to work independently when required.
- A friendly, courteous and relaxed manner, coupled with a careful and rigorous approach to research work.
- The ability to speak a foreign language would be an advantage.

Training

Half day general induction course including the museum's Front of House Code of Practice. Specialist training covering interviewing and observation of visitors, the process of exhibit development, and ethical practices in social science at the Science Museum.

The National Museum of Science & Industry is an equal opportunities employer.

Appendix F

Volunteer recruitment information and forms

Volunteer Programme

AT THE SCIENCE MUSEUM

sci√m
SCIENCE
MUSEUM

The Science Museum's Volunteer Programme has a rewarding exciting experience in store for you

sci√m
SCIENCE
MUSEUM

Science Museum
Exhibition Road
London SW7 2DD
Tel: 0171 938 8008
Minicom Line: 0171 938 9770
Disabled Person's Enquiry Line: 0171 938 9788
Open Daily: 10.00 to 18.00
Nearest Tube: South Kensington

The Volunteer Programme Office
Science Museum
Exhibition Road
London
SW7 2DD

Recruitment

We recruit volunteers who have a commitment to learn and wish to support the Science Museum. We then endeavour to match the skills and expertise of individual volunteers to appropriate positions as they arise.

All our volunteers are required to commit themselves to a minimum of 15 hours voluntary service each month.

Training

The Science Museum is committed to training and staff development. All volunteers will be provided with induction training and specialist training for each specific job.
Additional, on-going specialist sessions are offered for long term projects.

Skills and Experience

The volunteer programme encourages volunteers to develop new skills and learn from their experiences.

If you already have specialist skills which you believe could be of use to the Museum please tell us. We may call on your skills as new projects arise.

Opportunities

New volunteer opportunities occur regularly with new gallery projects and visitor events. Each volunteer opportunity has an accompanying job description and training programme. The current opportunities are listed on the insert.

To apply for a volunteer position please complete a Volunteer Application Form. Application Forms and job descriptions are available from the Volunteer Programme Office on 0171 938 8028.

Volunteer Programme

The Volunteer Programme at the Science Museum will foster mutual support, personal development and learning—we stress the importance of volunteering for the benefit of both the Museum and the volunteer.

Volunteer service offers an opportunity for a diverse group of volunteers to provide skills, support and commitment of time to the Museum. This is given in exchange for training, education and a host of new experiences.

If you are aged sixteen or over and would like to become involved with some exciting new projects going on in the Science Museum then we should like to hear from you.

Volunteer Application Form

Please complete **all sections**

Personal details

Title (circle one)					Surname	Forenames
Dr	Mr	Mrs	Miss	Ms		

Home Address	Contact address—*in emergency*

Daytime telephone number	Evening telephone number	Telephone number—*in emergency*

Date of birth	Town of birth	Nationality

Employment status (circle as appropriate)

Paid Employee	Volunteer Employee	Unemployed	Retired	Student

Where did you hear about the volunteer programme (circle as appropriate)

The Science Museum	the press	a friend	other

Why have you chosen to apply to become a science museum volunteer?

What volunteer position or area of work would you like to be considered for?

Science Museum   Exhibition Road   London   SW7 2DD

Employment history (last two positions held-voluntary or placements included)

Dates	Position held and principal duties	Name and address of employer

Education (last two courses completed)

Dates	Course completed	Place of study or training

Experiece, training or other voluntary work relevant to application

Dates	Details

Referees (please name two referees not related to you)

Name		
Telephone		
Address		

Declaration

I declare that the information I have given is true to the best of my knowledge

Signature   Date

Appendix G.1

Template for induction training programme for volunteers

This template provides a structure for a volunteer training programme. It should be developed for each specific volunteer position. Each individual volunteer will, of course, have their own personal training needs agreed and carried out in conjunction with the Manager of Volunteer Programmes.

Museums: what? and why? and how?

What: history of the Science Museum

- Slide show and talk on the history and development of the Science Museum.

Why: aims and objectives of the Science Museum

- Mission and core objectives.
- Collecting: What to collect.
- Educating: Learning and teaching from collections.
- Exhibiting: Interpreting and displaying collections.
- Conserving: The science and art of conservation.

How: the Science Museum's activities

- *Public Affairs Division*: the Customers' Charter and the Front of House Code of Practice; the Trading Company.
- *Science Communication Division*: the process of exhibition research and development; visitor events programmes; the activities and services provided by the education staff.
- *Collections Division*: how to create a collection; the uses of a national collection; research; the role of a conservator.
- *Resource Management Division*: sources of income; expenditure; managing resources.

Appendix G.2

Introduction to *Volunteers' Handbook*

Welcome

Welcome to the Science Museum's Volunteer Programme. We are delighted to have you as a volunteer and hope that the experience will be enjoyable and rewarding for you and the museum.

This handbook, together with training, will provide you with a general introduction to the Science Museum. We aim to supply you with sufficient information to prepare you to carry out your duties and fulfil your responsibilities as a Volunteer.

You will be asked to tell us about your experience as a volunteer by completing a questionnaire. The responses that you give to the questions are essential for the development of the programme and will benefit future volunteers.

Practicalities of working as a volunteer in the Science Museum

Access to the museum and your work place

On each day that you work as a volunteer you should make yourself known to your supervisor. This is primarily for your own safety and for security purposes. It allows the museum to know exactly who is in the building in the case of an evacuation.

Most volunteer positions will require you to draw keys from the Control Room in order to gain access to your work place. These keys are the property of the museum. They must be signed for and acknowledged on return. Keys should *never* be lent to anyone else or taken outside the museum building.

On your first day as a museum volunteer you will be met by a member of staff and advised on basic administrative procedures.

Your personal possessions and valuables

Please avoid bringing valuables into the museum as we cannot be held liable for their loss. If you do have to bring something of value into the building, please ask a member of staff for their advice on the safest place to store it.

Your safety

Your safety is paramount. For health and safety purposes you will be treated like a permanent member of staff.

You should not attempt to carry out any task which may endanger yourself, the public, or any other member of staff. Some tasks that you may consider to be simple may have health and safety implications when performed in a National Museum. For example, familiar tasks such as fixing a loose door handle, changing a light bulb or issuing an elastoplast to a visitor may only be carried out by fully trained and appointed staff: Joiners, electricians and first aiders respectively. If you are in doubt about carrying out any task, ask a member of staff.

Evacuation

In the event of an evacuation, listen carefully to the announcement on the tannoy and follow the instructions as if you were a member of the public. Do not attempt to clear the building of visitors and/or staff yourself; this is the responsibility of the Warding Team.

On evacuating the museum it is essential that you assemble outside the Imperial College and Science Museum Libraries with other museum staff and make your presence known to the Manager of Volunteer Programmes or your supervisor for that day. It is their responsibility to ensure that you are safely out of the building. On no account re-enter the building until your supervisor has advised you that it is safe to do so.

Dress code

All museum staff, paid and voluntary, are expected to dress smartly each day and wear a Science Museum name badge as provided. It is important that you are readily identified by the visitors and the staff. We expect you to wear a name badge and follow the dress code at all times. Please bear in mind that the museum may vary in temperature from one gallery or office to the next.

If you are working in a designated 'Front of House' position, you will be provided with a sweatshirt or t-shirt with the Science Museum logo on the front and the title 'volunteer' on the back. The sweatshirt or t-shirt will be lent to you for the duration of your deployment in the museum. Volunteers are expected to provide for themselves and wear: navy or black trousers or skirt, navy or black shoes and, a plain white shirt, blouse or t-shirt. Please avoid jeans as there are many shades and you may be mistaken for a visitor.

Your responsibility as a Science Museum volunteer

You are responsible for turning up on the day that you agreed to work, or informing The Volunteer Programme Office that you are unavailable at least one week in advance. In the case of sickness, or other unforeseen absence, please endeavour to call The Volunteer Programme Office as soon as you are aware that you are no longer available to work. An answer machine will receive your message 24 hours a day.

Appendix H

Volunteers' Agreement

1 I undertake to attend the museum as reasonably required by the demands of the work or project on which I have been engaged.

2 I agree to inform my supervisor as soon as possible should I be prevented from attending the museum for any reason, e.g. sickness.

3 I accept that when working as a volunteer at the Museum I will work under the guidance of my supervisor.

4 I have read and fully understand all the instructions and regulations regarding security, health and safety, fire and other emergency evacuation procedures. I am also aware that the museum has a no smoking policy.

5 I accept that should I breach any instructions or act a way incompatible with the image of the museum my engagement may be terminated.

6 I agree to take part in induction programmes as required by the museum prior to working as a volunteer and to undergoing performance assessments during that period of working. In the event of my being unable to achieve the required standard for any reason I agree to withdraw from the engagement.

7 I understand that I am entitled to free admission to the museum throughout the period covered by the agreement.

8 I agree to taking breaks from duty as a volunteer in the designated rest areas provided for that purpose. I also agree to keeping all personal belongings in the secure areas provided for volunteers by the museum.

9 I agree to sign an attendance register on each day I come to work as a volunteer.

10 I accept responsibility for all tools, equipment and protective clothing made available to me for the duration of the agreement.

11 In the event of dispute or grievance arising with the museum I agree to abide by the procedures laid down by the museum.

12 I accept that this agreement is valid for the period .... to .... and that any subsequent renewal of the agreement is made at the discretion of the museum.

13 I accept that I am entitled to ask the museum for a reference based on my service as a volunteer if I wish to do so.

14 I understand that I will be eligible for staff discount on purchases in the Museum's refreshment areas and in the Museum Shop whilst working as a volunteer.

Declaration

I understand and accept the terms and conditions of the Science Museum's Volunteers' Agreement as set out above.

Volunteer

Signature　　　　.................................... *Date* ....

Name　　　　.....................................

Address　　　　.....................................

Volunteer Position ....

Manager of Volunteer Programmes

Signature　　　　.................................... *Date* ....

References and further reading

AAM (1984) *Museums for a New Century: A Report on the Commission on Museums for a New Century* (Washington, DC: American Association of Museums).

—— (1989) *Evaluation in a Museum Setting* (Washington, DC: American Association of Museums Professional Committee on Visitor Evaluation).

—— (1992) *Excellence and Equity* (Washington, DC: American Association of Museums).

—— (1993) *Museums, Adults, and the Humanities: A Guide to Educational Programming* (Washington, DC: American Association of Museums).

—— (1994) *Code of Ethics for Museums* (Washington, DC: American Association of Museums).

Abidi, A., Ali, A., Barrett, P., Barron, S., Duffin, P., Fairhead, A., Genner, R., Haddow, P., Harrison, P., Kendall, A., Philpotts, A., Salim, A., Shen, S. and Tallent, G. (1976) *The Pimlico Connection* (London: Department of Electrical Engineering, Imperial College).

Adair, J. (1987) *Not Bosses but Leaders* (London: Kogan Page).

Adirondack, S. (1992) *Effective Management for Voluntary Organisations and Community Groups* (London: London Voluntary Service Council).

Alexander, E. (1979) *Museums in Motion* (1907) (Nashville, TN: American Association for State and Local History).

Allen, V. L. (ed.) (1976) *Children as Teachers* (London: Academic Press).

Alt, M. B. and Griggs, S. A. (1984) 'Psychology and the museum visitor' pp. 386–93 in J. M. A. Thompson (ed.) *Manual of Curatorship: A Guide to Museum Practice* (London: Butterworth).

Ambrose, T. (ed.) (1987) *Education in Museums, Museums in Education* (Edinburgh, Scottish Museums Council: HMSO).

Ambrose, T. and Runyard, S. (eds) (1991) *Forward Planning: A handbook of business, corporate and development planning for museums and galleries* (London: Routledge).

Anderson, D. (1995) 'Gradgrind Driving Queen Mab's Chariot: what museums have (and have not) learnt from adult education' pp. 11–33 in A. F. Chadwick and A. Stannett (eds) *Museums and the Education of Adults* (Leicester: National Institute of Adult and Continuing Education).

—— (1997) *A Common Wealth: Museums and Learning in the UK* (London: Department of National Heritage).

Anderson, L. L. (1991) 'Zoo interpretation and exhibit design: two sides of the same coin' *Journal of Museum Education* 16. 2: 4–6.

Anslow, A., Elliot, M., Hibbs, M., Posner, D., Rushmer, J. and Siddiqui, D. (1977) *The Pimlico Connection: Phase 2* (London: Department of Electrical Engineering, Imperial College).

Argentini, J. (1989) *Practical Corporate Planning* (London: Unwin Hyman).

Argyle, M. (1996) *The Social Psychology of Leisure* (London: Penguin).

ASTC (1990) *What Research Says about Learning in Science Museums*. Vol. 1. (Washington, DC: Association of Science and Technology Centers).

—— (1993) *What Research Says about Learning in Science Museums*, Vol. 2 (Washington, DC: Association of Science and Technology Centers).

—— (1994) *Vision to Reality: Critical Dimensions in Science Centre Development*, Vol. 2 (Washington, DC: Association of Science and Technology Centers).

Audit Commission (1991) *The Road to Wigan Pier? Managing Local Authority Museums and Art Galleries* (London: HMSO).

BAFM (1994) *Are You Insured?* (London: British Association of Friends of Museums).

—— (1995) 'Volunteers training day' *British Association of Friends of Museums Newsletter* 54: 5.

de Bakker, L. (1995) 'The Pimlico Connection–Science Museum Project: An evaluation of the project from a science communication perspective' (unpublished M.Sc. dissertation, (Science Communication Unit, Humanities Programme, Imperial College, London SW7 2BX).

Barbe, C. (1989) 'Voluntary youth work camps for museums' *Museum* 163. 3: 188–91.

Barnes, B. (1985) *About Science* (Oxford: Blackwell).

Barnes, B. and Edge, D. (1982) *Science in Context: Readings in the Sociology of Science* (Milton Keynes: Open University Press).

Barrow, C. and Paul, J. (1988) *The Business Plan Workbook* (London: Kogan Page).

Bausell, R. B., Moody, W. B., and Walzl, F. N. (1972) 'A factorial study of tutoring versus classroom instruction' *American Educational Research Journal* 9: 592–7.

Beardon, T. (1990) 'Cambridge STIMULUS' Chapter 5 of S. Goodlad and B. Hirst (eds) *Explorations in Peer Tutoring* (Oxford: Basil Blackwell).

Ben-David, J. (1984) *The Scientist's Role in Society* (first published 1971) (London: University of Chicago Press).

Bennet, T. (1995) *The Birth of the Museum: History, Theory, and Politics* (London: Routledge).

Berry, N. and Mayer, S. (eds) (1989) *Museum Education: History, Theory, and Practice* (Virginia: National Art Education Association).

Bicknell, S. and Farmelo, G. (eds) (1993) *Museum Visitor Studies in the 90s* (London: The Science Museum).

Bitgood, S., Serrel, B., and Thompson J., (1994) in Crane, V. (ed.) *Informal Science Learning: What the Research Says about Television, Science Museums, and Community-based Projects* (Edinburgh: Scottish Museums Council).

Bloom, S. (1975) *Peer and Cross-age Tutoring in the Schools: An Individualised Supplement to Group Instruction* (Washington, DC: National Institute of Education) (ERIC Reproduction Service No. ED 118 543).

Blud, L. M. (1991) 'Social interaction and learning among family groups visiting a museum' *Museum Management and Curatorship* 9: 43–51.

Borun, M. (1977) *Measuring the Immeasurable: A Pilot Study of Museum Effectiveness* (Washington, DC: Association of Science and Technology Centres).

Borun, M., and Flexer, B. K. (1983) *Planets and Pulleys: Studies of Class Visits to Science Museums* (Washington, DC: Association of Science and Technology Centers).

Brindle, D. (1994) 'Bias bars young as voluntary workers' *Guardian* 2 June 1994.

Brownfoot, J. and Wilks, J. F. (1993) *Directory of Volunteering and Employment Opportunities* (London: Directory of Social Change).

Burns, E-K., (1996) 'Valuing volunteers in the heritage industry' *Volunteering* 15: 8.

Butler, S. (1992) *Science and Technology Museums* (Leicester: Leicester University Press, Leicester Museum Studies).

Butterworth, D. (1995) 'Deprived of work' *Volunteering* 8: 8.

Byrne, K. (1992) 'Friends of museums' (unpublished MA Thesis, Leicester University Library).

Cahalan, M. and Farris, E. (1990) *College Sponsored Tutoring and Mentoring Programs For Disadvantaged Elementary and Secondary Students* Higher Education Surveys – Report Number 12 (Washington DC : US Department of Education. Office of Planning, Budget and Evaluation) (ED323884).

Campbell, I. (1995) 'Student tutoring and pupil aspirations' Chapter 12 in S. Goodlad (ed.) *Students as Tutors and Mentors* (London: Kogan Page).

Carre, C. and Ovens, C. (1994) *Science 7–11: Developing Primary Teaching Skills* (London: Routledge).

Castle, M. C. (1996) 'Perspective transformation: the continuing education of the volunteer docent' paper presentation 'Special Interest Group on Education and Museums' *The XXIV Annual Learned Societies Conference* (Ontario: St. Catherine's) 5 June 1996.

Chadwick, A. F. (1980) *The Role of the Museum and Art Gallery in Community Education* (Nottingham: Department of Adult Education, University of Nottingham).

Chadwick, A. F. and Stannett, A. (eds) (1995) *Museums and the Education of Adults* (Leicester: National Institute of Adult and Continuing Education).

Clarke, C. (1992) 'Museums and volunteers towards success' (unpublished MA thesis Leicester University Library).

Cloward, R. A. (1967) 'Studies in tutoring' *Journal of Experimental Education* 36. 1: 14–25.

Cohen, J. (1986) 'Theoretical considerations of peer tutoring' *Psychology in the Schools* 23: 175–86.

Cohen, P. A., Kulik, J. A., and Kulik, C. C. (1982) 'Educational outcomes of tutoring: a meta-analysis of findings' *American Educational Research Journal* 19: 237–48.

Coles, A. (1996) 'Managing volunteers for visitor care' Association of Independent Museums *Focus* April 1996.

Conrad, E. E. (1975) '*The effects of tutor achievement level, reinforcement training, and expectancy on peer tutoring*' (unpublished Ph.D. thesis, University of Arizona, university microfilms No. 76, 1407).

Conway, L. (1994) *Working with Volunteers*

Handbook: Training (Berkhampstead: The Volunteer Centre).

Cornfield, M. , Keene, S. and Hackney, S. (eds) (1989) *Conservation Facilities in Museums and Galleries* (London: United Kingdom Institute for Conservation).

Cossons, N. (1984) 'Independent museums' pp. 84–90 in J. Thompson (ed.) *Manual of Curatorship* (London: Butterworth).

—— (1985) 'Making museums market-orientated' pp. 41–7 in Scottish Museums Council (ed.) *Museums are for People* (Edinburgh: Scottish Museums Council).

Cossons (1991) 'Class culture and Collections' pp. 13–24 in *The Museums Profession: Internal and External Relations* (Leicester: Leicester University Press)

—— (1991) 'Policy and style' pp. 6–9 in T. Ambrose and S. Runyard (eds) *Forward Planning: A handbook for business, corporate and development planning for museums and galleries* (London: Routledge).

Crane, V., Nicholson, H., Chen, M., and Bitgood, S. (eds) (1994) *Informal Science Learning: What the Research Says about Television, Science Museums, and Community-based Projects* (Dedham, MA: Research Communications Ltd.).

Csikszentmihalyi, M. and Hermanson, K. (1996) 'Intrinsic motivation in museums: why does one want to learn?' pp. 67–77 in J. H. Falk and L. D. Dierking (eds) *Public Institutions for Personal Learning* (Washington, DC: American Association of Museums).

CSV (1995a) *Learning Together: The Added Value of Student Tutors Volunteering in Schools* (London: Community Service Volunteers).

—— (1995b) *Learning Together: Student Tutoring – Research and Evaluation Papers on Pupil Aspirations and Student Tutor Skills* (London: Community Service Volunteers).

Danilov, V. J. (1991) *Corporate Museums, Galleries, and Visitor Centres: A Directory* (Westport, CN: Greenwood Press).

Davies, S. (1994) *By Popular Demand* (London: Museums and Galleries Commission).

Davis-Smith, J. (1993) *Volunteering in Europe: Opportunities and Challenges for the 90s* (Berkhampstead: The Volunteer Centre).

Demb, C. and Castle, C. (1994) 'Training the volunteer museum educator' pp. 41–52 in *Second Museum Education Colloquium* (Ontario: Ontario Museum Association).

Denver Museum of Natural History (1994) 'Volunteer and staff handbook' (unpublished; available from Denver Museum of Natural History, Denver, CO).

Department of National Heritage (1996) *Treasures in Trust* (London: Department of National Heritage).

Devin-Sheehan, L., Feldman, R. S., and Allen, V. L. (1976) 'Research on children tutoring children: a critical review' *Review of Educational Research* 46: 355–85.

Diamond, J. (1979) 'The social behaviour of adult–child groups in the science museum' (unpublished doctoral dissertation, University of California, Berkeley).

—— (1987) *The Exploratorium Explainer Programme: The Long-term Impacts on Teenagers of Teaching Science to the Public* (Chichester: John Wiley).

Diamond, J., St. John, M, Cleary, B., and Librero, D. (1987) 'The Exploratorium Explainer Program: the long-term impacts on teenagers of teaching science to the public' *Science Education* 71. 5: 643–56.

Drake, C. S. (1986) *How to start a Friends Association for your Museum or Art Gallery* (available from the British Association of Friends of Museums. Printed by courtesy of Robson Rhodes, Chartered Accountants).

Duensing, S. (1987) 'Science centres and exploratories: a look at active participation' in Ciba Foundation *Communicating Science to the Public* (Chichester: Wiley).

Durant, J. D. (1990) 'Copernicus and Conan Doyle: or why should we care about the public understanding of science?' *Science and Public Affairs* 5: 7–22.

—— (ed.) (1992) *Museums and the Public Understanding of Science* (London: Science Museum).

Eckstein, J. (ed.) (1992) *Museums and Galleries Funding and Finance: Cultural Trends* (London: Policy Studies Institute, 14.4.2).

Edwards, D. and Mercer, N. (1987) *Common Knowledge: The Development of Understanding in the Classroom* (London: Methuen).

Eisenberg, T., Fresko, B., and Carmeli, M. (1980a) *A Tutorial Project For Disadvantaged Children: An Evaluation of the PERACH Project* (Rehovot, Israel: Perach, Weizmann Institute of Science).

—— —— (1980b) *PERACH: A tutorial project for disadvantaged children* (Rehovot: The Weizmann Institute of Science).

—— —— (1981) 'An assessment of cognitive change in socially disadvantaged children as a result of a one-to-one tutoring program' *Journal of Educational Research* 74. 5: 311–14.

—— —— (1982) 'Affective changes in socially disadvantaged children as a result of one-to-one tutoring' *Studies in Educational Evaluation* 8. 2: 141–51.

—— —— (1983a) 'A follow-up study of disadvantaged children two years after being tutored' *Journal of Educational Research* 76. 5: 302–6.

—— —— (1983b) *The Effect at Different Grade Levels of One and Two Years of Tutoring* (Rehovot, Israel: Perach, Weizmann Institute).

Ellis, S. J. (1986) *From the Top Down* (Philadelphia: Energize).

—— (1990) *Proof Positive: Developing Significant Volunteer Record-keeping Systems* (Philadelphia: Energize).

Ellis, S. J. and Noyes, K. H. (1990) *By the People: A History of Americans as Volunteers* (San Francisco: Jossey-Bass).

Ellson, D. G. (1986) 'Improving productivity in teaching' *Phi Delta Kappan*, October: 111–24.

Ellson, D. G., Barber, L. W., and Harris, P. L. (1969) *A Nation-wide Evaluation of Programmed Tutoring* (Illinois: Department of Psychology, University of Indiana).

Ellson, D. G., Barber, L., Engle, T. L., and Kampwerth, L. (1965) 'Programmed tutoring: a teaching aid and a research tool' *Reading Research Quarterly* 1. Fall: 77–127.

Ellson, D. G. and Harris, P. L. (1970) *Project Evaluation Report: Programmed Tutoring on Beginning Reading New Albany Public School System 1969–70* (Mimeo) (Illinois: Department of Psychology, University of Indiana).

Ellson, D. G., Harris, P. L., and Barber, L. (1968) 'A field test of programmed and directed tutoring' *Reading Research Quarterly* 3. 3. Spring: pp 307–67.

Elsdon, K. T. with Reynolds, J. and Stewart, S. (1995) *Voluntary Organisations: Citizenship, Learning and Change* (Leicester: National Organisation for Adult Learning).

ERIC (Office of Educational Research and Improvement) (1988) *ERIC Database: College Students who Tutor Elementary and Secondary Students* (Washington, DC: US Department of Education).

Falconer, H. (1996) 'Freely given' *Museums Journal* June: 28–9.

Falk, J. H. and Dierking, L. D. (1992) *The Museum Experience* (Washington, DC: Whalesback Books).

—— —— (eds) (1996) *Public Institutions for Personal Learning* (Washington, DC: American Association of Museums).

Falk, J. H., Koran, J. J., and Dierking, L. D. (1986) 'The things of science' *Science Education* 70: 503–8.

Fasko, D. and Flint, W. W. (1990) *Enhancing Self-esteem of At-risk High School Students* (unpublished report, Kentucky, ED348593).

Feber, S. (1987) 'New approaches to science, in the museum or out with the museum' in T. Ambrose, (ed.) *Education in Museums, Museums in Education* (Edinburgh: Scottish Museums Council).

Feldman, R. S., Devin-Sheehan, L., and Allen, V. L. (1976) 'Children tutoring children: a critical review of research' Chapter 15 in V. L. Allen (ed.) *Children as Teachers* (London: Academic Press).

Fielding, N., Reeve, G., and Simey, M. (1991) *Active Citizens* (London: Bedford Square Press).

Finn, D. (1985) *How to Visit a Museum* (New York: Harry N. Abrams).

Fisher, J. (1986) *Handbook for Volunteer Organisations*, No. 5 (Ottawa, Canada: Voluntary Action Directorate).

Fisher, J. C. and Cole, K. M. (1993) *Leadership and Management of Volunteer Programs: A Guide for Volunteer Administrators* (San Francisco: Jossey-Bass).

Flaxman, E., Ascher, C., and Harrington,

C. (1988) *Youth Mentoring Programs and Practices*. (New York: Institute for Urban and Minority Education).

Fletcher-Brown, K. B. (1987) *The Nine Keys to Successful Volunteer Programs* (Washington, DC: American Association of Museums).

Follet, D. (1978) *The Rise of the Science Museum* (London: Science Museum).

Foot, H. C., Morag, M. J., and Schote, R. H. (eds) (1990) *Children Helping Children* (Chichester: Wiley).

Fresko, B. (1988) 'Reward salience, assessment of success and critical attitudes among tutors' *Journal of Educational Research* 81: 341–6.

Fresko, B. and Carmeli, M. (1990) 'PERACH: A nation-wide student tutorial project' Chapter 4 of S. Goodlad and B. Hirst (eds) *Explorations in Peer Tutoring* (Oxford: Basil Blackwell).

Fresko, B. and Chen, M. (1989) 'Ethnic similarity, tutor expertise and tutor satisfaction' *American Educational Research Journal*, 26. 1: 122–40.

Fresko, B. and Eisenberg, T. (1985) 'The effects of two years of tutoring on mathematics and reading achievement' *Journal of Experimental Education* 53. 4: 193–201.

Friedman, A. J. (1995) 'Differentiating science-technology centres from other leisure-time experiences' (paper presented at the ECSITE Conference 1995).

Fries, C. and Randon, A. (1993) *Facts and Figures on the Voluntary Sector*, Information Briefing No. 1 (London: National Council for Voluntary Organisation).

Fuchs, L. S., Fuchs, D., Bentz, J., Phillips, N. B., and Hamlett, C. L. (1994) 'The nature of student interactions during peer tutoring with and without prior training and experience' *American Educational Research Journal* 31. 1: 75–103 (Spring).

Gathercole, P. (1989) 'The fetishism of artefacts' pp. 73–82 in S. Pearce (ed.) *Museum Studies in Material Culture* (Leicester: Leicester University Press).

Glazer, J. S. and Wughalter, E. (1991) 'MENTOR in education: attracting minority students to teaching careers' *Mentoring International* 5. 1–2: 15–20.

Goodlad, S. (1973) *Science for Non-Scientists: An Examination of Objectives and Constraints in* the *Presentation of Science to Non-specialists* (Oxford: Oxford University Press).

—— (1975) *Education and Social Action: Community Service and the Curriculum in Higher Education* (London: George Allen & Unwin).

—— (1979) *Learning by Teaching* (London: Community Service Volunteers).

—— (ed.) (1982) *Study Service: An Examination of Community Service as a Method of Study in Higher Education* (Windsor: NFER-Nelson).

—— (1985) 'Putting Science into Context' *Educational Research* 27. 1: 61–7.

—— (ed.) (1995a) *Students as Tutors and Mentors* (London: Kogan Page).

—— (1995b) *The Quest for Quality: Sixteen Forms of Heresy in Higher Education* (Buckingham: SRHE and Open University Press).

—— (1996) *Speaking Technically: A Handbook for Professional Scientists, Engineers and Physicians on How to Improve Technical Presentations* (London: Imperial College Press).

Goodlad, S., Atkins, J., and Harris, J. (1978) *Undergraduates as School Science Tutors* (London: Department of Electrical Engineering, Imperial College).

Goodlad, S. and Hirst, B. (1989) *Peer Tutoring: A Guide to Learning by Teaching* (London: Kogan Page).

—— —— (eds) (1990) *Explorations in Peer Tutoring* (Oxford: Basil Blackwell).

Gordon, D. (1996) 'Bland new broadcast' *Prospect* March: 62–5.

Graff, L. L. (1993) *By Definition: Policies for Volunteer Programs* (Ontario, Canada: Volunteer Ontario).

Green, L. and Hughes, J. C. (1992) *Report of the 2nd BP National Workshop on Student Tutoring* (London: Imperial College).

Green, T. (1996) 'What specials want is to be valued' *Volunteering* 17. April: 6.

Gregory, R. (1986) *Hands-on Science: An introduction to the Bristol Exploratory* (London: Duckworth).

—— (1989) Keynote address in *Sharing Science* (London: Nuffield Foundation).

Grinder, A. L. and McCoy, E. S. (1985) *The Good Guide: A Source Book for Interpreters Docents and Tour Guides* (Scottsdale, AZ: Ironwood Publishing).

Hagstrom, W. O. (1965) *The Scientific Community* (London: Basic Books).

Hall, E. (1995) 'All for love' *Museums Journal* October: 25.

Happer, T. A. M. (1994) 'Volunteers can create as well as implement' *ASTC Newsletter* March/April: 9–10.

Harlen, W. (ed.) (1985) *Primary Science: Taking the Plunge* (London: Heinemann Educational).

Harrison, G. V. (1969) *The Effects of Trained and Untrained Tutors on Criterion Performance of Disadvantaged First Graders* (Los Angeles: University of California, ERIC No. ED 031 449).

—— (1971a) *Structured Tutoring* (Provo, UT: Department of Instructional Research and Development, Brigham Young University, ERIC No. 053 080).

—— (1971b) *How to Organise an Inter-grade Tutoring Program in an Elementary School* (Provo, UT: Brigham Young University Printing Service).

—— (1972a) *Supervisors' Guide for the Structured Tutorial Reading Program* (Provo, UT: Brigham Young University Press).

—— (1972b) 'Tutoring: a remedy reconsidered' *Improving Human Performance* 1. 4: 1–7.

Hayson, J. (1994a) *Science Sense* (Toronto: Ontario Institute for Studies in Education).

—— (1994b) *Science Sense Teachers' Guide* (Toronto: Ontario Institute for Studies in Education).

Hayward, D. G. and Jenson, A. D. (1981) 'Enhancing a sense of the past: perception of visitors and interpreters. *The Interpreter* 12. 2: 4–11.

Heaton, D. (1992) *Museums Among Friends: The Wider Museum Community* (London: HMSO).

Hector Taylor, M. (1992) *Report of the Sheffield Tutoring Scheme* (Sheffield: University of Sheffield Enterprise Unit).

Hedley, R. (1991) *Volunteering Today* (Berkhamstead: The Volunteer Centre).

Hedley, R. and Davis-Smith, J. (eds) (1992) *Volunteering and Society: Principles and Practice* (London: Bedford Square Press).

Hein, H. (1990) *The Exploratorium: The Museum as Laboratory* (Washington DC: Smithsonian Institution Press).

Hiemestra, R. (1981) 'The state of the art' pp. 61–72 in Z. W. Collins (ed.) *Museums, Adults, and the Humanities* (Washington, DC: American Association of Museums).

Hill, S. and Topping, K. (1995) 'Cognitive and transferable skill gains for student tutors' Chapter 11 of S. Goodlad (ed.) *Students as Tutors and Mentors* (London: Kogan Page).

Hirsch, F. (1977) *The Social Limits to Growth* (London: Routledge and Kegan Paul).

Hogget, P. and Bishop, J. (1986) *Organising Around Enthusiasms: Patterns of Mutual Aid in Leisure* (London: Comedia Publishing Group).

Holdsworth, N. (1994) 'Citizens' service idea for young people' *Times Educational Supplement* 3 June: 2.

Hooper-Greenhill, E. (1994) *Museums and their Visitors* (London: Routledge).

Hovland, C. I., Janis, I. L., and Kelly, H. (1953) *Communication and Persuasion* (Westport, CN.: Greenwood Press).

Hudson, K. (1975) *A Social History of Museums* (London: Macmillan).

—— (1992) *Prayer or Promise: The Opportunities for Britain's Museums and the People who Work in Them* (London: HMSO).

Hughes, J. C. (1991a) *Wicked, Brilliant, Radical: 16th Annual Report of the Pimlico Connection* (London: Imperial College).

—— (ed.) (1991b) *Tutoring Resource Pack* (Alton: BP Educational Service).

—— (1992) *My Happiest Moments at Imperial: 17th Annual Report of The Pimlico Connection* (London: Imperial College).

—— (1993) 'Student tutoring in North America' *Peer Tutoring Newsletter* 93: 6–7.

ICOM (International Council of Museums) (1990) *Statutes: International Council of Museums* (Paris: ICOM).

Jackson, E. T. and McNamara, J. E. (1987) *Issues and Opportunities* (Ottawa, Canada: Voluntary Action Directorate).

Jackson, L. and Bicknell, S. (1995) *Science Box: Information Superhighway Summative Evaluation* (London: Science Museum Public Understanding of Science Research Unit).

Jones, A. K. G. (1993) 'The role of unpaid staff in hands-on centres' *British Interactive Group Newsletter*.

Jones, J. (1989) *Effect of Student Tutors on School Students' Attitudes and Aspirations: Report to the Department of Education* (Auckland, Higher Education Research Office).

—— (1990) 'Tutoring as field-based learning: some New Zealand developments' Chapter 6 of S. Goodlad and B. Hirst (eds), *Explorations in Peer Tutoring* (Oxford: Basil Blackwell).

—— (1993a) 'University students as tutors in secondary schools' in: *Proceedings of a Conference on Peer Tutoring at the University of Auckland New Zealand 19–21 August 1993*, (Higher Education Research Office and University of Auckland).

—— (ed) (1993b) *Peer Tutoring: Learning by Teaching* (proceedings of Auckland Conference on Peer Tutoring, August 1993).

Jury, L. (1994) 'Reaching out' *Guardian* 25 May 1994: 12.

Kalfus, G. R. (1984) Peer mediated intervention: a critical review *Child and Family Behaviour Therapy* 6. 1. Spring: 17–43.

Kavanagh, G. (ed.) (1991) *The Museums Profession: Internal and External Relations* (Leicester: Leicester University Press)

Kelly, B. (1986) 'The volunteer as professional' *American Association of Museum Volunteers News*. Winter.

Klaus, D. J. (1975) *Patterns of Peer Tutoring* (Washington, DC: American Institutes of Research, National Institute of Education Project No. 4–0945).

Klosterman, R. (1970) 'The effectiveness of a diagnostically structured reading program' *The Reading Teacher* 24: 159–62.

Knapp, M. (1990) *Time is Money: The Costs of Volunteering in Britain Today* (Berkhampstead: The Volunteer Centre).

Knapp, M., Koutsogeorgopoulou, V., and Davis-Smith, J. (1995) 'Who volunteers and why?

The key factors which determine volunteering' *ARVAC Bulletin* 61. Summer: 10–12.

Knight, B. (1993) *Voluntary Action* (London: Centris).

Kuyper, J., Hirzy, E., and Huftalen, K. (1993) *Volunteer Program Administration: A Handbook for Museums and other Cultural Institutions* (New York: AAMV and American Council for the Arts).

Lalande, C. (1989) *Volunteer Management* (Sudbury, Ontario: a Science North).

Last, J. (1993) Foreword of *Museum Sector Workforce Survey: An Analysis of the Work in the Museums, Galleries, and Heritage Sector in the United Kingdom*, prepared by the Management Centre, Bradford for the Museums Training Institute (London: Museums Training Institute).

Latour, B. (1987) *Science in Action: How to Follow Scientists and Engineers through Society* (Milton Keynes: Open University Press).

Layton, D., Jenkins, E., Macgill, S., and Davely, A. (1993) *Inarticulate Science* (Driffield, Yorks: Studies in Education).

Leach, J., Driver, R., and Scott, P. (1994) 'The nature of science: young people's representations' *Education in Science* April: 20–1.

Levin, H. M., Glass, G. V. and Meister, G. R. (1987) 'Cost-effectiveness of computer-assisted instruction' *Evaluation Review* 7. 1. February: 50–72.

Lewin, A. (1992) 'Research that supports informal learning' *Hand to Hand* 6. 2: 1–10.

Lewis, J. (1984) 'Collections, collectors, and museums: a brief world survey' in J. M. A. Thompson (ed.) *Manual of Curatorship* (London: Butterworth).

Locke, S. (1991) 'Growing pains' *Museums Journal* December: 30–2.

Logan, R. N. S. (1991) 'Guides in the flesh – and all volunteers' *Museum* 169. 1: 52–53.

Loomis, R. J. (1986) *Museum Visitor Evaluation: New Tool for Management* (Washington, DC American Association for State and Local History).

Lynn, P. and Davis-Smith, J. (1991) *The 1991 National Survey of Voluntary Activity in the United Kingdom* (Berkhampstead: The Volunteer Centre).

McCarty, D. (1994) 'V = TWS (Volunteering = Time Very Well Spent)' *Science Scope Newsletter* 4. 2: 1 (San Diego Space and Science Foundation).

McCurley, S. and Lynch, R. (1994) *Essential Volunteer Management: A Directory of Social Change Publication* (London: Directory of Social Change).

Macduff, N. (1991) *Building a Short-term Volunteer Program: Episodic Volunteering* (Lincoln, Wala Wala, WA: MBA Publishing).

McManus, P. (1987) 'It's the company you keep. . . . The social determination of learning-related behavior in a science museum' *International Journal of Museum Management and Curatorship*.

—— (1993) 'Thinking about visitors' thinking' in S. Bicknell and G. Farmelo (eds) *Museum Visitor Studies in the 90s* (London: The Science Museum).

—— (1994) 'Families in museums' Chapter 6 of R. Miles and L. Zavalo (eds) *Towards the Museum of the Future* (London: Routledge).

Mann, M. (ed.) (1995) 'Volunteering is a job-seeking activity' *Volunteering* 6: 2.

Martin, M. (1994) *Virtuous Giving: Philanthropy, Service, and Caring* (Bloomington, IN: Indiana University Press).

Marton, F. and Saljo, R. (1976a) 'On qualitative differences in learning: outcome and Process' *British Journal of Educational Psychology* 46: 4–11.

—— (1976b) 'On qualitative differences in learning: II Outcomes as a function of the learner's conception of the task' *British Journal of Educational Psychology* 46: 115–27.

Mason, D. (1991) 'Questioning the unquestion-able' in T. Ambrose (ed.) *Money, Money, Money and Museums* (Edinburgh: Scottish Museums Council/HMSO).

Masters, R. (1993) *Beyond Relativism: Science and Human Values* (London: University Press of New England).

Matsushita, T. (1991) 'In Japan: the volunteers of the National Science Museum' *Museum* 171. 3: 144.

Mattingly, J. (1984) *Volunteers in Museums and*

Galleries: The Report of a Survey into the Work of Volunteers in Museums and Galleries in the UK (Berkhampstead: Berkhampstead Volunteer Centre).

Mauss, M. (1950) *The Gift: Forms and Functions of Exchange in Archaic Societies* (London: Cohen & West).

Melaragno, R. J. (1976) *Tutoring with Students: A Handbook for Establishing Tutorial Programs in Schools* (Englewood Cliffs, NJ: Educational Technology Publications).

Melton, A. W., Feldman, N. G., and Mason, C. W. (1988) *Experimental Studies of the Education of Children in a Museum of Science* (Washington, DC: American Association of Museums).

Meltzer, P. (1989) 'Help them help you' *Museum News* March/April: 60–2.

Merriman, N. (1991) *Beyond the Glass Case* (Leicester: Leicester University Press).

Middleton, V. T. C. (1991) 'The future demand for museums 1990–2001' pp. 12–29 in G. Kavanagh (ed.) *The Museum Profession* (Leicester: Leicester University Press).

Miles, R. (1987) 'Museums and the communication of science' pp. 114–22 in Ciba Foundation *Communicating Science to the Public* (Chichester: John Wiley).

Miles, R. and Tout, A. (1989) 'Exhibitions and the public understanding of science' pp 27–33 in J. R. Durant (ed.) *Sharing Science* (London: Nuffield Foundation).

Millar, S. (1991) *Volunteers in Museums and Heritage Organisations: Policy, Planning and Management* (Office of Arts and Libraries, London: HMSO).

Moore, L. (1985) *Motivating Volunteers* (Vancouver, Canada: Vancouver Volunteer Centre).

Museum of Science, The (1993) 'Museum of Science annual report 1992–93' (unpublished; available from the Museum of Science, Boston, MA).

Museums Association (1992) *Museums Association Annual Report 1992/93* (London: Museums Association).

NCVO (1993) *Facts and Figures on the Voluntary Sector* (London: National Council of Voluntary Organisations).

Neate, J. (1995) *Quality Through Volunteers* (Berkhampstead: The Volunteer Centre).

Niedermeyer, F. C. (1970) 'Effects of training on the instructional behaviors of student tutors' *Journal of Educational Research* 64. 3: 119–23.

Nielsen, M. (ed.) (1988) *A Directory of Museum Volunteer Programs* (Washington, DC: American Association of Museum Volunteers).

Niyazi, F. (1996a) *Volunteering by Older People* (London: The National Centre for Volunteering).

—— (1996b) *Volunteering by Young People* (London: The National Centre for Volunteering).

—— (1996c) *Volunteering by Disabled People* (London: The National Centre for Volunteering).

—— (1996d) *Volunteering by Unemployed People* (London: The National Centre for Volunteering).

—— (1996e) *Volunteering by People with Disabilities* (London: The National Centre for Volunteering).

Nuffield Foundation (1989) *Sharing Science* (London: Nuffield Foundation).

Oakland Museum of California, The (1985) *Extending Connections* (California: The Oakland Museum of California).

—— (1994a) 'The docent defined' (A comprehensive manual compiled by the Docent Council; California: The Oakland Museum of California).

—— (1994b) 'Guide to the Oakland Museum' (publicity leaflet/flyer; The Oakland Museum of California).

Oakland Museum Docent Council (1994) 'You grow, we grow', (leaflet; The Oakland Museum of California).

Office of Arts and Libraries (1991) See Millar, S. (1991).

Olofsson, U. K. (1979) *Museums and Children* (Paris: UNESCO).

O'Neill, M. (1991) 'After the artefact: internal and external relations in museums' in G. Kavanagh, (ed.) *The Museum Profession* (Leicester: Leicester University Press).

Paolitto, D. P. (1976) 'The effect of cross-age

tutoring on adolescence: an inquiry into theoretical assumptions'. *Review of Educational Research* 46. 2. September: 215–37.

Parker, S. (1983) *Leisure and Work* (London: George Allen & Unwin).

Pearce, S. (ed.) (1996) *Exploring Science in Museums* (London: Athlone).

PERACH Central Office (1984) *PERACH 1974–1984: Ten Years of Tutoring* (Rehovot, Israel: The Weizmann Institute of Science).

Pinkston, C. N. (1993) 'The volunteer bridge' *Museum News* May/June: 56–7.

Pitkeathley, J. (1993) *Working with Volunteers Handbook: Support* (Berkhampstead: The Volunteer Centre).

Pizzey, S. (ed.) (1987) *Interactive Science and Technology Centres* (London: Science Projects).

Potter, J. (1995) 'New directions in student tutoring: the UK experience' Chapter 10 of S. Goodlad (ed.) *Students as Tutors and Mentors* (London: Kogan Page).

Prince, D. R. and McLoughlin, H. (1987) *Museums UK: The Findings of the Museums Data Base Project* (London: Museums Association).

Quin, M. (1990) 'The Exploratory pilot a peer tutor? The interpreter's role in an interactive science and technology centre' Chapter 13 of S. Goodlad and B. Hirst (eds) *Explorations in Peer Tutoring* (Oxford: Basil Blackwell).

Rainbow, M. (1992) 'A volunteer programme: the Hutchison report' *Muse* 9. 3: 36–8.

Ravetz, J. J. (1971) *Scientific Knowledge and its Social Problems* (Oxford: Clarendon).

Rawlings-Jackson, V. and Shaw, P. (1995) *Paying Attention: A Guide to Customer Care in the Arts* (London: The Arts Council of England).

Regnier, K., Gross, M, and Zimmerman, R. (1992) *The Interpreter's Guidebook: Techniques for Programs and Presentations* (Stevens Point, WI: UW-SP Foundation Press Inc., University of Wisconsin).

Reisner, E. R., Petry, C. A. and Armitage, M. (1990) *Review of Programs Involving College Students as Tutors or Mentors in Grades K-12*, Vols I and II (Washington, DC: Policy Studies Institute) Department of Education.

Richter, M. N. (1973) *Science as a Cultural Process* (London: Frederick Muller).

Roger, L. (1987) 'Museums in education: seizing the market opportunities' in T. Ambrose (ed.) *Education in Museums, Museums in Education* (Edinburgh: Scottish Museums Council).

Royal Society, The (1985) *The Public Understanding of Science* (London: The Royal Society).

Salmon, D. (ed.) (1932) *The Principal Parts of Lancaster's 'Improvements' and Bell's 'Experiment'* (Cambridge: Cambridge University Press).

Science North (1993) 'Science North annual report 1992/93' (unpublished; available from Science North, Sudbury, Ontario).

—— (1994a) 'Visitors guide 1994/95' (unpublished; available from Science North, Sudbury, Ontario).

—— (1994b) 'Science North strategic plan, 1994–95, 1996–97' (unpublished; available from Science North, Sudbury, Ontario).

Scottish Museums Council (1985) *Museums are for People* (Edinburgh: HMSO).

Screven, C. G. (1986) 'Exhibitions and information centers: some principles and approaches' *Curator* 182: 553–9.

Seaborne, M. (1966) *Education: The History of Modern Britain* (London: Studio Vista).

Serrell, B. (ed.) (1990) *What Research Says about Learning in Science Museums*, Vol. I (Washington, DC: Association of Science and Technology Centers).

—— (ed.) (1993) *What Research Says about Learning in Science Museums*, Vol. II (Washington DC: Association of Science and Technology Centers)

Sharp, M. N. and Shremp, M. (1992) 'United States: volunteers lead the way' *Museums* 176: 230–3.

Shaver, J. P. and Nuhn, D. (1971) 'The effectiveness of tutoring under-achievers in reading and writing' *Journal of Educational Research* 65: 107–12.

Shettel, H. H. (1973) 'Exhibits: art form or

educational medium?' *Museum News* 52. 9: 32–41.

Shore, M. (1995) 'Students as tutors in early childhood settings' Chapter 14 in S. Goodlad (ed.) *Students as Tutors and Mentors* (London: Kogan Page).

Shortland, M. (1987) 'No business like show business' *Nature* 328: 213.

Smith, D. R. (1994) *Working with Volunteers Handbook: Recruitment and Selection* (Berkhampstead: The Volunteer Centre).

Smithers, A. and Robinson, P. (1989) *Increasing Participation in Higher Education* (London: BP Educational Service).

Smithsonian Institute (1994) *Official Guide to the Smithsonian* (Washington, DC: Smithsonian Institute Press).

Solinger, J. W. (1990) *Museums and Universities: New Paths for Continuing Education* (New York: American Council on Education/Macmillan).

Spalding, J. (1991) 'Is there life in museums?' in G. Kavanagh, (ed.) *The Museum Profession* (Leicester: Leicester University Press).

Standing, I. (1992) 'Volunteer training' *Association of Independent Museums Newsletter* August. 15: 4.

Stedman, H. J. (1990) 'Museums and universities: partners in continuing education' Chapter 11 in J. W. Solinger (ed.) *Museums and Universities: New Paths for Continuing Education* (New York: American Council on Education/Macmillan).

Stewart, D. W. and Shamdasani, P. N. (1990) *Focus Groups – Theory and Practice* (Newbury Park: Sage).

Swagerman, J. (1991) 'Volunteer guides: a condemned species' *Museum* 172. 43. 4: 193–6.

Tait, S. (1989) *Palaces of Discovery: The Changing World of Britain's Museums* (London: Quiller Press).

Taylor, S. (1986) *Understanding Processes of Informal Education: A Naturalistic Study of Visitors to a Public Aquarium* (unpublished doctoral dissertation: University of California, Berkeley).

Thomas, A. and Finch, H. (1990) *On Volunteering: A Qualitative Research Study of Images, Motivations, and Experiences* (Berkhampstead: The Volunteer Centre).

Topping, K. (1988) *The Peer Tutoring Handbook* (Beckenham: Croom Helm).

Topping, K. and Hill, S. (1995) 'University and college student as tutors for schoolchildren: a typology and review of evaluation research' Chapter 2 in S. Goodlad (ed.) *Students as Tutors and Mentors* (London: Kogan Page).

Townley, B. (1994) *Reframing Human Resource Management* (London: Sage).

Tremper, C. and Kostin, G. (1993) *No Surprises: Controlling Risks in Volunteer Programs* (Washington, DC: Non-Profit Risk Management Center).

Trivulzio, A. (1990) 'Volunteers and the role of the museum for schools, the handicapped and hospitals' *Museum Management and Curatorship* 9: 273–90.

Uzzell, D. (1993) 'Contrasting psychological perspectives on exhibition evaluation' in S. Bicknell and G. Farmelo (eds) *Museum Visitor Studies in the 90s* (London: The Science Museum).

Valentine, D. (ed.) (1994) *Museums and Galleries in Great Britain and Ireland* (East Grinstead: Reed Information Services).

Velarde, G. (1992) 'Exhibition design' Chapter 67 in J. M. A. Thompson (ed.) *Manual of Curatorship: A Guide to Museum Practice* (London: Butterworth-Heinemann).

Volunteer Centre, The (1990) *Guidelines for Relations between Volunteers and Paid Workers* (Berkhampstead: The Volunteer Centre).

—— (1992) *Volunteers: Recruitment, Training, and Support* (Berkhampstead: The Volunteer Centre).

—— (1994a) *Volunteers Week 94: Resource Pack* (Berkhampstead: The Volunteer Centre).

—— (1994b) *Volunteering Matters* (Berkhampstead: The Volunteer Centre).

—— (1994c) *Volunteers on Management Committees* (Berkhampstead: The Volunteer Centre).

Warts, D. (1986) 'Professional volunteers: a contradiction in terms' *Museum Quarterly* Winter: 7–11.

Washburn, W. (1990) 'Museum exhibition' in M. S. Shapiro (ed.) *The Museum: A Reference Guide* (Westport, CN: Greenwood).

Whitcher, A. (1992) *Making the Right Choice: Guidelines on Selecting Volunteers* (Berkhampstead: The Volunteer Centre).

Whitcher, A. and McDonough, A. (1992) *Volunteers First: A Guide to Employment Practice: The Personnel Responsibilities of People who Manage Volunteers* (Berkhampstead: The Volunteer Centre).

Whitley, P. (1980) *An Enquiry into Study Service in Institutions of Higher Education* (London: Department of Education and Science and Community Service Volunteers).

—— (1982) 'Study service in the United Kingdom: a survey' Chapter 3 in S. Goodlad (ed.) *Study Service: An Examination of Community Service as a Method of Study in Higher Education* (Windsor: NFER-Nelson).

Wilkes, R. (1975) *Peer and Cross-age Tutoring and Related Topics: An Annotated Bibliography*, Theoretical Paper No. 53 (Madison, WN: Wisconsin Research and Development Center for Cognitive Learning, University of Wisconsin).

Wilson, M. (1976) *Effective Management of Volunteer Programs* (Colorado: Volunteer Management Association).

—— (1990) *Survival Skills for Managers (1981)*, fifth edition (Colorado: Management Associates).

—— (1992) 'Marlene Wilson challenges museum volunteer managers' *American Association of Museum Volunteers* 11. Winter: 17–31.

Winterbotham, N. (1994) 'Emphasis on enquiry' *Museums Journal* March: 18.

Wolfgang, A. (1992) *People Watching Across Cultures* (Ontario: Ontario Institute of Applied Psychology).

Wynne, B. (1991) 'Knowledge in context' *Science, Technology and Human Values* 16: 111–21.

Young, L. and Goulden, S. (1995) *The Science Museum Mystery Shopping Project* (London: MSS/Research International Limited).

Ziman, J. (1984) *An Introduction to Science Studies* (Cambridge: Cambridge University Press).

Index

131